INTERNATIONAL SOCIALISM

A quarterly journal of socialist theory

Spring 19

Content

Issue 66 of International Socialism, quarterly journal of the Socialist Workers Party (Britain)
Published March 1995

Distribution/subscriptions: International Socialism, PO Box 82, London E3.

American distribution: B de Boer, 113 East Center St, Nutley, New Jersey 07110.

Subscriptions and back copies: PO Box 16085, Chicago, Illinois 60616

Editorial and production: 071-538 1626/071-538 0538

Sales and subscriptions: 071-538 5821

American sales: 312 666 7337

ISBN 1 898876 08 8

Printed by BPC Wheatons Ltd, Exeter, England
Typeset by East End Offset, London E3

Cover design by Ian Goodyer

Subscription rates for one year (four issues) are:

Britain and overseas (surface):	individual	£14.00 ($30)
	institutional	£25.00
Air speeded supplement:	North America	nil
	Europe/South America	£2.00
	elsewhere	£4.00

Note to contributors
The deadline for articles intended for issue 68 of *International Socialism* is 20 March 1995.

All contributions should be double-spaced with wide margins. Please submit two copies. If you write your contribution using a computer, please also supply a disk, together with details of the computer and programme used.

INTERNATIONAL SOCIALISM ★

A quarterly journal of socialist theory

RUSSIA'S CRISIS reached new depths with Boris Yeltsin's bloody suppression of Chechnya. He won the battle but may have lost the war to hold on to his presidency. Dave Crouch writes from Moscow, assessing the liberals' political, economic and social record and showing how they have prepared the ground for forces to their right, including Russia's increasingly vociferous Nazi organisations. Finally he looks at how workers' organisations are placed to resist the rise of the right.

LAW AND ORDER have been the watchwords of the right in the industrialised countries for a generation. Social Democratic and Labour parties seem to have accepted the right's terms of debate—just at the moment when the United States is experiencing a catastrophic failure in law enforcement. American socialist Phil Gasper provides a devastating exposé.

BRITISH POLITICS is dominated by the rightward shift of Tony Blair's 'new look' Labour Party and the continued crisis of the Tory government. Alex Callinicos reviews the poverty of the Labour modernisers' thought and Judy Cox examines the withering of Tory party membership. Taking the longer view, Eric Hobsbawm's panorama of the 20th century, *Age of Extremes*, informs and infuriates in not quite equal measure, argues John Rees.

MATEWAN **IS** one of the finest films about working class struggle. John Newsinger pays tribute to its maker, John Sayles, but also uncovers the equally heroic struggles which surrounded the events that made it to celluloid. *International Socialism* 61 opened a debate on jazz. Here Charlie Hore brings the discussion to a close with a reply to his critics, whose views appeared in *International Socialism* 64.

IRISH POLITICS are obviously at a turning point. Pat Riordan's *Bookwatch* provides a guide.

The crisis in Russia and the rise of the right

DAVE CROUCH

As I finish this article, Russian television is broadcasting pictures of the Chechen capital, Grozny, in the north Caucasus, making parallels with the level of damage to Stalingrad in 1943. Thousands have died under the carpet of Second World War fragmentation bombs dropped from the air. Boris Yeltsin's Security Council is pumping out lies equal in their iniquity to the depths of Soviet propaganda during the Afghan war: the Chechens are supposedly blowing up the city, throwing babies out of windows, raping school teachers and castrating prisoners, while the Moscow press is all in their pay. The government has been starkly revealed to millions as a camouflaged politburo, led by the remote, disoriented figure of Boris Yeltsin. A postscript is being written into the Soviet Union's bloody history of imperial aggression, the first major chapter in the 'new' Russia's military aspirations.

Yeltsin's firmest supporter in the Chechen war is a Nazi—Vladimir Zhirinovsky. The spectacular failure of market reform in Russia has led to a rapid growth of Nazi organisations, among which Zhirinovsky's is the best known. This is an unpalatable conclusion, however, for the Western liberal establishment, who persist in referring to him as merely an aberration: 'mad Vlad', a 'right wing populist', 'brute patriot' and so on. Those who gave an ecstatic welcome to the wholesale application of the free market in Russia are naturally loath to admit that the collapse of these policies could threaten a rerun of the 1930s.

Many on the left in Britain and elsewhere are also confused about the Nazi right in Russia. For large numbers of socialists from Trotskyists to left social democrats the real fascist bogeymen are Yeltsin and the democrats, responsible for destroying the USSR, unleashing local nationalisms and forcing through the restoration of capitalism. Thus in October 1993 Ken Livingstone and the *New Statesman*, among others, defended vice-president Rutskoi and speaker Khasbulatov in their clash with the government, despite the latter's reliance on extreme Russian nationalists, anti-Semites and armed, *sieg-heiling* Nazis in their attempt to take the Kremlin by storm.[1] Boris Kagarlitsky, a Russian theorist of social democracy well known to the Western left, has been calling Yeltsin a fascist ever since August 1991, while accepting the alliance of old style Communists with extreme nationalists as a potentially left wing force.[2] This knee jerk reaction, however, only confuses cause with effect.

An understanding of the rise of the Russian right is important in several respects. Firstly, there can be few clearer examples of the madness of the market system that has driven millions to despair across the former USSR. While opinion polls show that hatred of the former Communist regime runs deep, there is bitter alienation from Yeltsin and the champions of liberal economics who have presided over the quite obscene enrichment of the ruling class—the former *nomenklatura*—and a small number of financial parasites, at the same time condemning ordinary Russians to unspeakable misery. With each slowdown in the pace of collapse they claim to see a light at the end of the tunnel, yet each small breathing space is followed relentlessly by another gut wrenching spiral of inflation, slump and unemployment. In the absence of a powerful challenge to this process from below the Nazis have begun to fill the political vacuum.

Secondly, for a left largely demoralised by the 'defeat of socialism' at the hands of the East European masses, it is vital to grasp the reasons for the collapse of those regimes and to see that they represented no obstacle whatsoever to the horrors that are now unfolding in their place. In this sense the relative strength of the Russian Nazis, their origins in the old regime and their close links with its staunch defenders today are chilling confirmation of the analysis of Soviet Russia long associated with this journal.[3] The contradictions of Russian state capitalism are unresolvable in the context of the international economic crisis, thereby creating the potential for a right wing backlash.

The dynamic of the situation in Russia today is not one way. The last few years in Western Europe have also seen the re-emergence of a Nazi threat, but simultaneously a faltering but at times explosive development of workers' struggle which has repeatedly thrown the Nazis back. The purpose of this article is to draw attention to a very real threat in Eastern Europe, to locate this threat in the failure of the market, and to assess the social forces that can resist it.

The failure of the Democrats—the economy

The logic pushing the Russian ruling class towards integration into the world market has already been analysed in detail over the last 30 years by Tony Cliff, Chris Harman and others.[4] Suffice to say that by the mid-1980s the internal contradictions of the command system had reached acute proportions with zero growth and the various elements of the economy irresponsive to central control, provoking yet another attempt at reform (Gorbachev had little original to offer—his was the fifth *perestroika* since Stalin died).[5] For the Russian bureaucracy, measures of decentralisation, of which market mechanisms have been a major element ever since they were touted by Malenkov in the mid-1950s, aimed to replace administrative with financial discipline at management level.[6] In the words of Georgy Khizha, the boss of a large military factory in St Petersburg who was brought into the government in May 1992: 'Either administrative fear or material interest. There is no fear any more'.[7]

For six years the Russian leadership shuffled towards the market, hemmed in by the fear of losing control while driven on by the worsening crisis. The coup attempt of August 1991 was made by those in the ruling class who looked to China and South Korea as their model: market reforms under tight dictatorial control. As finance minister and coup leader Pavlov admits:

> *By the early 1990s we had worked out a theory and mechanism of market transformation. We followed so-called 'salami tactics'...to gradually, bit by bit, in an evolutionary manner slice sector after sector away from central planning and transfer them to a market regime.*[8]

The beginning of 'shock therapy' in January 1992 marked a temporary speed up but not a radical break in this process. With Yeltsin's popularity riding high after the coup, the young academic economist Yegor Gaidar, who had only left the Communist Party that August, was brought in to front a 'kamikaze cabinet' which, on 1 January 1992, freed prices on all but a few essential goods. Free market theory quickly clashed with hard reality. The Russian economy is highly monopolised, over half of industrial output coming from 1,000 large firms employing an average of 8,500 workers.[9] Autonomy simply allowed producers to jack up prices. In the words of Sergei Glaziev, minister of finance under Gaidar but now a fervent oppositionist:

Prices changed not so much under the influence of supply and demand, but instead were dictated by the monopolised parts of the market. And in so far as the majority of enterprises had no alternative supplier they were forced to accept almost any price rise on the resources they used. Prices are determined in most cases by the seller, and not the buyer. Thus a change in price on the output of one enterprise elicits a proportional change in price throughout the entire technological chain, with the restoration in a short time of the original relation.[10]

As a result, prices shot up, sometimes way above those on the world market, leading inevitably to a fall in output and the build up of company debt. There was one way of stopping this process: open up the economy to international competition, thereby forcing firms to charge a competitive price. According to the economic liberals this was to have a positive side: ineffective firms were to go bankrupt, thereby increasing the effectiveness of the economy as a whole. As the then finance minister and ultra-liberal Boris Fyodorov put it in 1993, 'I am not one of those who takes pride in the slow-down in the industrial slump'.[11] But in a super-monopolised economy the bankruptcy of a few key firms has a knock-on effect throughout the rest of the country. As the *Washington Post* observed, 'The government cannot take such a step [ie to push through bankruptcy law] without condemning millions to unemployment. In certain circumstances entire cities built around a single large firm will die'.[12]

Even *Izvestiya*, the trumpeter of market reform, got cold feet:

It is hardly wise to close down monopoly producers, especially if they produce raw materials or intermediate products, because after this all the users of their products along the technological chain will inevitably collapse. It is very difficult to identify among the vast number of loss making firms a few, the bankruptcy of which will not be devastating.[13]

Thus in the summer of 1992 the government backed down from its intentions and began massive financial support to cover industrial debts. At first it promised 500 billion roubles, which rapidly became 1 trillion and ended up as 3 trillion roubles. The result, as one economist put it, was rather like taking a sleeping pill and a laxative at the same time: the controls were taken off industry, while the printing presses kept churning out endless credit, leading to another leap in inflation.

Economic policy since then has had nothing to do with the 'monetarism' so beloved of Gaidar, Fyodorov and the IMF. Instead the government has balanced between winding up the pressure on industry by opening up to international competition, thereby effecting a gradual reorientation toward the priorities of the world market, while simultaneously stepping in to bail out the economy when things get critical. As Yevgeny Yasin, economic adviser to Gorbachev and Yeltsin and economics minister from October 1994, put it, the difference between the government's economic policies under Gaidar in 1992 and under Chernomyrdin in 1994 was that Gaidar promised not to give industry any money, but did, while Chernomyrdin promised to give money, but didn't.[14] Changes in government personnel have therefore been largely cosmetic, designed to influence international lending and aid agencies, and have tended simply to bring government rhetoric in line with its actual practice. After the marketeers Gaidar and Fyodorov resigned at the end of 1993, for example, the *Financial Times* declared it 'the greatest disaster since Versaille' and predicted hyperinflation,[15] yet in a few months inflation had fallen to its lowest level for three years.

The economic reforms have been all shock and no therapy. By May 1994 output was officially at 44 percent of its 1990 level and set to fall by another 16 percent in 1995 (following a fall of 19 percent in 1992 and 12 percent in 1993). This average figure hides the catastrophic collapse of certain sectors, such as light industry (down to 25 percent of its level in 1990) and machine tool building (30 percent down). The slump has hit the high-tech sectors hardest of all. Thus in 1991-1992 the output of computer numerically controlled machine tools fell twelvefold. Investment is roughly at 30 percent of its 1990 level and falling rapidly—down in the productive sector by 57 percent in the first half of 1994 in comparison with the same period in 1993. The authoritative journal *Kommersant* concluded that Russia had entered a 'classical depression' and 'had taken on the obvious characteristics of a raw material economy'.[16]

So much for the 'therapy'. As for the shock, the official figures show that incomes have been halved since 1991. The average figure masks huge income differentials, with incomes of the richest 20 percent rising by 30 percent in the first half of 1994 alone, while those of the poorest fell by 15 percent. Bread and potatoes are the staple diet for millions of Russians. In December 1993 39.6 million people lived on incomes less than the official minimum, while 77 percent of the population lived on less than twice this sum. About 13 percent of the population (19.3 million) lived on less than necessary for biological existence. Unemployment is estimated by the International Labour Organisation to be four to five times higher than official figures—a total by mid-1994 of

4.5 million fully unemployed plus the same again on short-time working or on compulsory non-paid leave.[17]

Privatisation by means of vouchers has meant—as originally intended—a further concentration of wealth and control in the hands of the privileged few, as workers with a pitiful number of shares have naturally opted to sell. As *Finansoviye Izvestiya* reported:

> *In the majority of enterprises in Russia a large owner is appearing, or has already appeared. Today it is they who are taking control.*[18]

Over half Russia's GNP is now produced in the 'private' sector, but the dependence of private firms on state-run utilities is still almost total.

At the same time corruption and speculation have been given a free rein. As the liberal economist Grigory Yavlinsksy aptly put it, 'Our biggest mistake was that we freed this essentially mafia-like system from society, when we should have freed society from the system'.[19] Traders in non-ferrous metals on the stock exchange, for example, can make 2,000 percent profit in a week. The *Washington Post* estimates that up to $40 billion has been taken out of the country since 1991 and stashed in foreign banks. Instead of going to productive investment, government subsidies have been pocketed by directors and used to gamble on the financial markets. Yeltsin himself admits that bosses are paying themselves up to 10 million roubles a month—30 times the average wage and 100 times the wage of many factory workers.[20] There has always been a colossal gap between rich and poor in Russia: the first Soviet millionaires appeared in the 1930s at a time when the average monthly wage was under 200 rubles. But the crisis today has enabled the rapid accumulation of extraordinary sums. The rich have so much cash they don't know what to do with it: Moscow now has the highest concentration of casinos in Europe. The scrabble for wealth has led to daily gangland killings in the city.

With such obvious luxury cheek by jowl with abject poverty, it is quite understandable that Zhirinovsky's promise to hang mafiosi in public places can find a hearing.

The failure of the Democrats—the empire

Yeltsin and the Democrats are not merely responsible for the immiseration of the Russian population. They have also blazed a trail for the authoritarian right by encouraging Russian nationalism in economic, military and foreign policy. Russia has simply not 'capitulated to Western imperialism' after the end of the Cold War: on the contrary, after a series of defeats at the hands of the Soviet population, the Russian leadership has systematically fought to claw back its position as a world military and economic superpower.

This is clear first and foremost from the economic statistics. Far from handing over the rights of Russian companies and mineral riches to foreign investors, Yeltsin has followed a fairly protectionist course. Thus in 1992 the government turned down major Western companies and granted rights to the *Shtokmanovskoye* gas field in the Barents Sea, the richest in the area, to a consortium of 19 elite Russian defence firms. In 1993 the massive gas monopoly *Gazprom* announced that it 'categorically rejects the involvement of Western investors in major projects'. Similarly, an international tender for rights to the Udokan copper deposits, the largest in the world, was won by a Russo-Chinese firm in which the Russians had a controlling interest, against competition from BAP, Mitsubishi, Phelps Dodge and RTZ.

Little wonder, then, that by the end of 1994 the only major foreign involvement in the oil sector remained that of Conoco, which had invested a mere $300 million. Despite government attempts to attract foreign investment, by December 1993 the latter totalled only $7 billion, of which Germany accounted for 60 percent and the US for a mere 5 percent. Thus by the end of 1994 foreign capital in Russia was no more than that invested in Estonia alone![21] When compared with the $109 billion dollars invested by Japan in the US by 1990, it is clear that Russia remains economically 'independent' of the West, while the latter is unlikely to risk investment in such a politically unstable region.

Russia has also run into stiff tariff barriers imposed by the US and the European Union, which are worried that cheap exports will drive prices down in an already depressed world market. One area, however, in which Russia has been actively carving itself out an international role is arms sales. Although in the last few years Russian weapons exports have almost halved and bring less than a quarter of the earnings of natural gas exports,[22] from the end of 1992 the liberal press devoted more and more attention to the restoration of military production. In January 1993 presidential adviser Mikhail Malei announced that the government is observing a 'new concept', according to which the defence sector will not destroy the country, but rather feed it. 'Whether or not this pleases the pacifists,' he said, 'this is the law of the market'.[23] A month later Yeltsin announced:

> *Not long ago I was in India, and I began to doubt that it is necessary to reduce military production. There is a colossal market there for our military products, and then we wouldn't have to re-convert defence factories back from saucepan production.*[24]

In recent years Russia has concluded a series of major arms contracts with India, China, Iran, Turkey and the Middle Eastern countries, all in the face of stiff US competition and, in the case of the sale of rocket motors to India, the threat of a 50 percent reduction in US economic aid.[25] In October 1994 defence minister Grachev announced that military-civil conversion should be stopped altogether in favour of a massive increase in arms sales.[26] In this area, Yeltsin's government is simply fulfilling one of Zhirinovsky's main demands.

Russia has also gradually increased its military presence in the countries of the former USSR, seeking to overcome its 'Afghan syndrome', the domestic population's hostility to the use of Russian troops since the defeat in Afghanistan.

Yeltsin made his intention clear right from the start. On 26 August 1991 (less than a week after the coup attempt) Yeltsin's press secretary announced a possible revision of Russia's borders: the Russian leadership sent the Ukraine and Kazakhstan a note threatening to annex territory in these republics if they didn't sign a new Union Agreement.[27] Here the leadership of the 'new' Russia fairly accurately repeated the calls of the far right *Soyuz* group of parliamentary deputies led by Colonel Alksnis, who threatened to take Latgalia from Latvia, the Virumaa region in north east Estonia, and to annex north Kazakhstan. In fact, Russia's leaders clearly went beyond their *Soyuz* companions. On 27 August 1991 Gavriil Popov, then the mayor of Moscow, appeared on television talking not only about possible annexations of the Crimea and eastern Ukraine, but also Odessa, Izmail and virtually the entire Black Sea coast. Russia has kept up its military pressure on the Ukraine through its claims to the Black Sea fleet, which it wants in order to match the Turkish naval build up in the region.[28]

Yeltsin picked up where Gorbachev had left off in Tbilisi, 1989, Baku, 1990, and Vilnius, 1991. In November 1991 he decided to send in the tanks to crush the independence of Chechnya, the tiny but oil rich republic in the north Caucasus. Russian troops met such mass resistance that they turned and fled, the operation ending in a fiasco. From then until December 1994 Moscow acted more circumspectly, its intervention taking place under the flag of 'peacekeeping forces'. But the following pattern emerged: everywhere Russian troops constituted the bulk of the peacekeeping forces, they were brought in only after the main fighting had taken place and therefore had little positive influence on the severity of bloodshed, they showed a clear preference for one of the conflicting sides (or supplied both sides with weapons so as to exhaust their economies and force them towards Moscow), they often relied on local unofficial armed gangs, and everywhere they have left untouched the underlying problems originally provoking conflict.[29]

All the above listed elements were present in the Russian interventions in the Georgian republics of South Ossetia and Abkhazia, which enabled Russia to sign a deal in March 1994 resurrecting Russian military bases on Georgian territory. In the words of Zbigniew Brezhinski, the former US security chief, 'Just ask Shevardnadze [the Georgian leader] what he thinks about the sources of the [Abkhazian] conflict, and he'll tell you that the Russian army initiated the conflict and used it so that it could later say: we will mediate, but give us three large military bases on the Turko-Georgian border'.[30] The pattern was faithfully repeated in the puppet Dnestr Republic (Moldova) in July 1992, which vice-president Rutskoi called Russia's Grenada,[31] and again in North Ossetia in November the same year, when Russia chose to back the local regime in driving 70,000 Ingushis from their homes in the area near Vladikavkaz that had been annexed from Ingushetia by Stalin in 1944. A taste of what happened after the arrival of Russian 'peacekeepers' is given by an eyewitness journalist's report:

> *The Ossetian volunteers tumbled out of their cars, formed a line and set off along the village street, raking the houses and yards with fire. On a few gates white rags marked Ossetian homes, which were left alone. As for the others—the gate is kicked in and they open fire in the corridor. Petrol is thrown on the walls, a match, and it explodes in flame. And the line moves on. A kick, bullets, explosion, flame. Kick, bullets, explosion, flame...*[32]

North Ossetia was then turned into a military outpost for Russia in the Caucasus, with a quantity of arms per head of population the highest in the world.[33] It was from its Ossetian bases that Russia launched its second attempt to invade Chechnya in December 1994. Since the fiasco of 1991 Moscow had kept up economic and military pressure on Grozny, looking for an opportunity to unseat its leader, General Dudayev, and put a more compliant figure in his place. In the summer of 1994 a direct threat to Russian hegemony in the Caucasus appeared in the shape of Azeri claims to the fabulously rich oil fields of the Caspian Sea and its moves to involve British, US and Turkish oil companies in developing the reserves. Pipelines from Baku run through Georgia and Armenia, already within the Russian ambit, and through Grozny, which is also the site of major oil refineries. In September Azerbaijan dropped a bombshell by including Iran in a deal to reroute oil to the south, threatening Russia's pipeline monopoly. (see the map on p14, below)

Bringing Chechnya to heel became an economic and strategic necessity for Moscow, which stepped up its funding of the Chechen military opposition. Ruslan Khasbulatov, himself a Chechen and leader of the October 1993 attempt to storm the Kremlin, was given Russian cash and arms to increase Moscow's influence and establish himself as opposition leader. The Federal Counter-Intelligence Service, successor to the KGB, recruited Russian officers to fight in Chechnya. Doku Zavgayev, Chechnya's former Communist boss overthrown by a popular uprising in September 1991 after backing the Moscow coup leaders, was brought into Yeltsin's administration and put forward as a leading candidate to take Dudayev's place.

After the failure to invade Grozny using proxy forces, Yeltsin opted for a full scale mobilisation of Russian troops and razing Chechen villages and the centre of Grozny to the ground, which earned him the active support of Zhirinovsky and much of the extreme right. In the meantime, the three year long civil war with the Islamic opposition in Tadjikistan continues, with the involvement of 25,000 Russian troops.

Moscow's growing confidence to assert its claim to the role of military policeman in the former Soviet bloc has been accompanied by a general hardening of its foreign policy. In 1992 statements by leading government figures about 'friendly relations' with Iraq and calls for sanctions against Croatia allowed *Izvestiya* to talk of 'a clear drift in the foreign ministry's approach' to foreign policy as a whole.[34] In March 1993 Yeltsin announced, 'The moment has come when the respective international organs should grant Russia special powers as the guarantor of peace and stability on the territory of the former Soviet Union'.[35]

The discovery in early 1994 of a Russian spy, Aldridge Ames, in the leadership of the CIA dramatically confirmed that Moscow was continuing its former Cold War behaviour. In the UN and the CSCE Russia and the US have increasingly clashed over Yugoslavia and the role of the NATO alliance in Eastern Europe.

If Russia is really flexing its imperial muscles, how are we to view the end of the Cold War, the collapse of the USSR and Russia's initial orientation on the US?

When *perestroika* began, the USSR's improved relations with the West were dictated by the economic crisis which had been bearing down on the country since the late 1970s. In the words of Sergei Karaganov, deputy director of the Russian Academy of Science's Institute of Europe and member of Yeltsin's Presidential Council:

> *The Soviet leadership tried to break out of the system of confrontation that had built up as a result of the Cold War and which was extremely unfavourable to the USSR. The Soviet Union with its weak and unreliable satellites was forced to stand up to a coalition of the world's most advanced countries. Moreover, by the end of the 1970s it was clear to many in Moscow that the 'buffer' created by Stalin in the countries of Central and Eastern Europe offered no real security but was very costly... Finally, the East*

> *European empire was expensive in the direct sense—Moscow spent enormous sums on subsidising neighbouring countries.*[36]

But in addition to these negative considerations, there were also positive factors pushing the politburo to reform its relations with the outside world, namely the 'desire to achieve access to the Atlantic markets for technology'.[37] According to the Reform Foundation of Stanislav Shatalin and Vadim Bakatin, the Soviet leadership hoped that by losing its status as the imperial metropolis it would make big economic gains.[38] As Ruslan Khasbulatov put it in 1991, 'Another factor was leading to the creation of a braking mechanism in the economy—the transformation of productive isolationism into autarchy, isolation from the world market...[the consequence] of the destructive concept of "absolute independence" from the world market'.[39]

The 'destructiveness' for the Soviet economy of 'absolute independence from the world market' followed from the inability of a single country—even one as large as the Soviet Union—to match world technological progress in all spheres. The Russian oil sector provides a good example. The US giant Amoco recently proposed joint drilling in the complex *Priobsky* oilfield with the Russian firm YuNG, offering to split the gain 20 to 80 with the Russian side. Apart from this obvious financial incentive to the Russian state, reluctant to exploit the *Priobsky* field without the US firm's financial might and drilling technology, and on top of Amoco's readiness to contract out the rig construction to major Russian producers, Russia also needs to turn its newly privatised 'seven sisters' into world class competitors in the oil business:

> *Without the* **Priobsky** *contract YuNG is likely to get nowhere. Only such a project can attract big investment like a magnet, enabling a breakthrough in oil refining and petrochemicals. Russia cannot afford the luxury of middle-category oil companies and average pipelines. This is...a question of geopolitics.... The new independent states of the post-Soviet south are trying to re-orient the flow of raw materials (mainly oil and gas) to by-pass Russia.* [On the other hand,] *major contracts and deals will bind them to traditional markets, co-operative links and sales routes.*[40]

Thus according to the original plan, sloughing off its Soviet imperial skin should have enabled Russia to leap ahead economically. Of course, no one at the top expected the empire to blow up in their faces—a consequence of 60 years of national oppression at Russian hands. On top of that, the world slump meant that no one was eager to welcome Russia into the world market. This is why the balance sheet of *perestroika* for the Russian ruling class has been so negative.

However, as the above discussion reveals, there was no 'capitulation' to the Americans. When the Russian ruling class stopped reeling from the defeats inflicted on it by the population after 1989 it set about strengthening its position both at home and abroad. The big show of post-Cold War friendship between Russia and the US was necessary to

both sides. The Kremlin needed to persuade its people that the bad old days were over and that reform would take them to an affluent market future:

> *Reformers in these* [East European] *countries do not invite foreign advisers because they do not know what to do. They invite them in order to clearly mark the direction of the course of reform. Moreover, in the eyes of the educated public, an authoritative Western adviser can put an important 'seal of approval' on any new reforms.*[41]

Bush and Clinton, on the other hand, could scarcely continue to talk of a Communist threat, and they constantly admonished American workers for complaining while the Russians were prepared to suffer so much just to duplicate the US market system.[42] In fact, US 'humanitarian aid' to Russia was a tiny drop in the ocean, and almost all of it came with strings attached, such as stipulations to pay US transport firms to deliver the aid.[43] General US acquiescence to Russia's proposed role as policeman in its backyard points to fears of the possible 'Yugoslavisation' of Eastern Europe. As Clinton himself put it, 'Imagine the consequences for Europe if millions of Russian citizens decide that they have no other option than to flee to the West'.[44]

Indeed, it is an open question whether or not US imperialism has 'gained' much from the collapse of the USSR.[45] Talk of an 'end of history' and the victory of 'liberal democratic' capitalism cannot disguise the crisis facing both Washington and Moscow. The latter's response to this crisis—the stepping up of imperial propaganda and the defence of 'Russian national interests'—is a mark of the failure of market reform, a major concession to the far right, and therefore an encouragement to it.

The failure of the Democrats—democracy

Nothing has done more to strengthen the trend towards authoritarianism than Yeltsin's record on democracy: he has disgraced the concept and fed the yearning for a 'firm hand' to restore order.

When Yeltsin stepped onto a tank outside the Moscow White House on the afternoon of Monday 18 August 1991 to lead the opposition to the coup, he dramatically asserted his image as the champion of democracy against Communism. The ensuing battle on the streets was a very real battle against a very real enemy: the programme of the State Committee for the State of Emergency announced a ban on all 'meetings, street demonstrations, and also strikes'. Tens of thousands of Muscovites risked their lives to stop the tanks. Those politicians, however, who spent the coup safely locked up in the parliament, acted in sharp contrast with their professed democratic ideals. As Gavriil Popov wrote a year after the coup, the Russian leadership traded support for Yeltsin with concessions to leading figures in the state and the army, such as General Grachev, who were wavering: 'Considering that the storming of the White House [by Grachev's crack troops] didn't take place and that Grachev became Russian minister of defence, it is easy to conclude that both sides honoured their obligations to the full. In the future it will be clear how many more such negotiations took place'.[46]

Instead of pushing home the victory over the putchists, Yeltsin did everything in his power to restrain the crowds on the streets and to make sure that there were no repeats of the 1989 scenes in East Berlin, for example, when thousands stormed the building of the Stasi (secret police) and seized files. Popov adds in this respect:

> *Yeltsin's main contribution as a politician is that he completely rejected the idea of turning the victory over the* [putchists] *into a wholesale purge of the former system, into a revolution of the Leninist type... In contrast to the leaders of the Russian Revolution of 1917, who were personally absolutely hostile to the former Russian ruling class, Yeltsin could see the reform-minded sections of the party and other Soviet structures as a potential reserve... Without the support of the Russian president I, as mayor of Moscow, could never have restrained the 'revolutionary' anger of the masses.*[47]

Immediate indications of how shallow were the changes that Yeltsin's victory brought about were the fact that no dissident figures were brought into government as in Eastern Europe.

Yeltsin's pragmatic attitude to democracy soon manifested itself. In November 1991 he postponed local elections and appointed governors to run local administrations, while his adviser Sergei Stankevich announced, 'A period of root-and-branch reform is no time for the flourishing of parliamentary democracy'.[48] Like Gorbachev before him, Yeltsin brought hardliners into his immediate entourage, creating the unaccountable and all powerful Security Council under the hawkish Yuri Skokov. Yeltsin went so far in taking power from parliament and concentrating it in his own hands that his new 1993 constitution enshrining presidential authority in law was welcomed by Zhirinovsky. In 1994 the renamed KGB and the police were given 'stunning new powers, about which the militia could only dream in pre-*perestroika* times, or even under the "firm hand" of Pugo [one of the August 1991 coup leaders]'.[49]

After the coup attempt the failure of reform to deal with the crisis quickly opened up splits among the Yeltsinites. Though dressed up in terms of democratic principle, even *Izvestiya* finally had to admit that the divisions in the leadership were nothing but 'a struggle for power'.[50] While the parliamentary opposition to Yeltsin made no secret of its fondness for authoritarianism, the president's supporters in turn continually referred to the need to limit democracy. Thus in the run up to the April 1993 referendum on presidential power *Izvestiya* ran a story headlined 'Authoritarian Government Is Better Than No Government', and argued that 'in situations like that in Russia we must seek our salvation in strict, even authoritarian government'.[51]

On 21 September 1993 Yeltsin disbanded parliament, which had been elected during the high point of the pro-democracy movement in 1989 and 1990. In the morning of 4 October tanks began shelling the White House—an isolated civil war raged in the centre of Moscow for a day.[52]

In the aftermath of the fighting censorship was introduced and papers appeared with blank spaces. A two week state of emergency in the capital saw a curfew imposed and the army given a free hand. According to official figures a staggering 89,250 Muscovites were arrested during this period—almost 1 percent of the city's population. Many of them were beaten up and abused. The army and militia led pogroms against blacks from the southern republics and drove 9,776 people out of the city, the vast majority non-Russians.[53]

After the October events the Democrats renewed their calls for an end to democracy. Gavriil Popov announced:

> *I believed and believe now that the parliamentary system in its classical, all-embracing, popular form is unacceptable for Russia in the transition period... The bourgeois countries that have gone through similar stages of development had no systems of direct universal suffrage.*[54]

Valeria Novodvorskaya, the outspoken leader of the Democratic Union, recommended 'enlightened authoritarianism' under Yeltsin, because 'the people are not ready for full democracy'.[55] A year later the leading liberal daily *Segodnya* declared that voting rights should be restricted to 5 to 10 percent of the population:

> *The country needs order, and not a parliament for good marks in some Council of Europe or other. Once again we must repeat the well-known truism: in a mad-house the doctors are not elected.* [56]

Given the close similarities between the government's policies for the economy, the empire and democracy, and the frequency with which leading Yeltsinites have defected to the opposition, it is hardly surprising that Yeltsin's leadership has compromised with the Russian nationalists, and vice versa. Rather than face civil war within the bureaucracy again spilling onto the streets, Yeltsin soon agreed to an amnesty for his opponents in October 1993. Though Yeltsin has yet to resort openly to the nationalist card, he has made conciliatory gestures to the Nazis and brought extreme right figures into the government. Thus in February 1994 the nationalities minister Sergei Shakhrai sent greetings and an offer of mutual co-operation to the World Congress of Russian Communes, well known for its Nazi sympathies.[57] The press minister Boris Mironov was forced to resign in September 1994 after a scandal concerning his demands for a centralised, government controlled media, and for his remark, 'I am a strict nationalist. Internationalism is the devil's invention. If Russian nationalism is fascism, then I am a fascist'.[58] After his sacking Mironov went straight to join General Sterligov's

Russian National Assembly. But Mironov joined the government as protégé of the speaker of the upper house Shumeiko and the information minister Poltoranin. Poltoranin, a leading member of Gaidar's party, 'Russia's Choice', has made little secret of his nationalist and anti-Semitic sympathies, announcing to a Jordanian newspaper that Russia was at risk of occupation by Zionist forces and declaring in a television interview that the Russian press talked in 'the Hebrew of the prison camps' and was 'Russophobic'.[59]

The war in Chechnya brought home the underlying similarity between Yeltsin and the opposition, especially when Yeltsin's only backing was from Nazis and Boris Fyodorov's tiny liberal fraction. The government commissioned Alexander Nevzorov—scandalous monarchist and darling of the right who lost public favour when he made a film praising the 1991 invasion of the Baltic States—to make a film of Chechnya to 'correct the information balance' in Russian media reporting of the war.[60]

As a result of this betrayal by Yeltsin and the Democrats, democracy has become a tainted word in Russia and the system of electoral participation has been discredited, leading to disillusion and political apathy on a grand scale. At Russia's first multi-party general elections in December 1993 only 53 percent of the electorate bothered to vote. At city wide local elections in Russia's second city, St Petersburg, in March 1994 the vote had to be extended for a second day while cars with loudspeakers toured the streets and electoral rights were suddenly granted to students and soldiers in order to achieve the statutory minimum 25 percent turnout.

The shift in public attitudes to Yeltsin was already clear by October 1993. In August 1991 the great majority of Muscovites who came to face the tanks were also uncritically pro-Yeltsin. But by the time of the next coup the numbers prepared to defend him were minimal. A few days later Alexander Minkin, the popular journalist for *Moskovsky Komsomolets*, wrote, 'People came [in answer to Gaidar's call for assistance]. Not out of love for Yeltsin and Gaidar, but out of contempt for Khasbulatov, Makashov and Anpilov [the coup leaders]'.[61]

The combination of rapidly worsening living standards with passivity and disillusionment in the Democrats led to a growing nostalgia for the past and a search for scapegoats among the national minorities. This was summed up by *Nezvisimaya Gazeta* straight after Zhirinovsky's election success in December 1993:

> *Did the Democrats really think that their hurriedly adopted wolf's clothing would look more attractive to the chauvinist electorate than the tried and*

> *tested mask of Zhirinovsky's party? Did they really think that they could shell their own parliament and at the same time command a majority?*[62]

Who are the Russian Nazis?

The Nazi label is a controversial one, both in Russia and elsewhere. Nazism differs from other reactionary movements firstly in terms of its *core social base in the middle class*, caught between the hammer and the anvil of the workers and the bosses, and secondly through its attempt to mobilise this social base into a *mass fighting force directed against workers*.[63] When Nazism is in its early stages, therefore—as it is in many countries of Western Europe today—these two distinguishing features are present only in embryo and hard to identify conclusively. Nor do reactionary movements go forward on some smooth and ever rising path to absolute power; they suffer set backs and crises, which also affect their leaders and their politics, making them twist, turn, hesitate and regroup. Furthermore, the scale of social conflict in Europe is not yet anywhere near that of Germany of the early 1930s or Italy after the First World War, so today's Nazis are often careful to mask their true intentions as they fight for political hegemony on the right. Finally, many would argue that the world has changed so much since the inter-war period that it is foolish to talk of a repeat of the 1930s, a social crisis of such catastrophic magnitude is ruled out, and that today's extremists are therefore merely playing at Nazism.

The situation in Russia today confirms, however, that the depth and intensity of social crisis have created perhaps the greatest social potential for a Nazi resurgence in Europe, along with a large number of individuals and organisations consciously attempting to go down Hitler's road.

The following survey of the Nazi right in Russia and the social milieu in which it is trying to build does not pretend to be comprehensive. There are approximately 90 extreme right newspapers in Russia today representing their own respective groupings.[64] Here we shall only look at the main ones.

Zhirinovsky—Russia's Le Pen

On 12 December 1993, barely two months after government tanks had shelled the parliament building in Moscow, Russians went to the polls for the first multi-party general elections since the civil war. Late that same evening millions tuned in to watch the sumptuous TV extravaganza organised by Boris Yeltsin's cabinet to celebrate its sweeping electoral victory. As the results came in, the show rapidly turned to farce: Vladimir Zhirinovsky, leader of the Liberal Democratic Party of Russia

(LDPR), had picked up nearly a quarter of the votes—the Democrats only 12 percent.

Zhirinovsky first appeared on the political scene during the Russian presidential elections of June 1991, when his promise to 'defend the rights of Russians in all territories' and ban all political parties won 6 million votes. By then he had already attracted the attention of other Russian Nazis, who saw him as a potential springboard into 'big politics'. Thus in spring 1991 Zhirinovsky appointed the leaders of the National-Social Union (NSU), Yuri Vagin and Victor Yakushev, to responsible posts in the LDPR in return for their assistance in his election campaign.[65] Vagin was known for his record as a monarchist dissident in the 1960s, while Yakushev was a leading member of *Pamyat* (the main Nazi outfit in the early years of *perestroika*), who declared in a 1991 interview that his political idols were Genghis Khan and Adolf Hitler.[66] At the time the NSU was a tiny Nazi grouping, one of several to emerge from *Pamyat*, looking for a means of building support.

The NSU left Zhirinovsky in early 1992. First it collapsed and then it re-formed as the National Front. Other Nazis had far a less casual and opportunistic relationship with Zhirinovsky. From 1991 his 'shadow cabinet' included two young Nazis, Andrei Arkhipov and Sergei Zharikov, soon to be joined by Eduard Limonov, who together played a determining role in the organisation's politics.

Arkhipov and Zharikov edited one of the LDPR's newspapers, *Sokol Zhirinovskovo* (*Zhirinovsky's Falcon*), and ran the party's uniformed and militarized youth wing, the Falcons. In 1992 and 1993 there were five issues of *Zhirinovsky's Falcon*, each with a print run of 50,000. Alongside regular articles by Zhirinovsky himself there is extensive material of a purely Nazi character, much of it written by Arkhipov and Zharikov themselves. A few quotes will suffice:

> *Today it is for some reason unacceptable to talk about the economic successes of the Third Reich, the cultural achievements that National Socialism gave the world. But no one can deny them!... Blood and soil are the two main principles of state formation; we need to form defence and storm groups, national socialist detachments. Russia is the last outpost of the white civilisation. We need a new racial genesis, as a result of which the caste of Russo-Slavs will revive the ancient Knowledge of Nature as an Aryan cosmos. The Day of the New White Race is dawning. We must form a United Nations of Peoples of the White Race. The final aim of Zionism is the economic and political domination of Jewry throughout the world and is the direct consequence of the national character of the Jewish people.*[67]

As the paper of the military wing of the LDPR, it was aimed at these core party activists, so talk of 'national socialist detachments' was not just wishful thinking.

But Zhirinovsky's reliance on these self confessed Nazis went much further than simply allowing them to edit his newspaper and educate his stormtroopers. Arkhipov and Zharikov had a key political role in the party. As Arkhipov remarked to the newspaper *Izvestiya*:

> *Almost all the slogans used by Zhirinovsky were thought up by myself and Zharikov. Ten minutes before he would speak to a crowd we would write out slogans in big letters, for example, 'America: give us back Alaska!' Zhirinovsky, in front of whom I would hold up the slogans, would then pick up on them and expand them.*[68]

This is not pure exaggeration: Arkhipov's statement is corroborated by Eduard Limonov in his book on Zhirinovsky,[69] which provides revealing insights into the LDPR. Limonov is a household name in Russia. A writer exiled in the Soviet period for his views, his return to Russia in 1992 coincided with the publication of his sexually explicit and semi-autobiographical novel *It's me, Eddy*, which was very popular among young people.

Limonov, Arkhipov and Zharikov split from Zhirinovsky in November 1992 to form the Right-Radical Party,[70] an openly Nazi outfit whose journal *Ataka* appears with a swastika on the cover. Limonov describes the split as follows: in September 1992 he and Zhirinovsky visited Le Pen in Paris:

> *Le Pen frowned* [and] *suddenly began to warn Zhirinovsky about 'young men in leather jackets who will pull your movement towards national socialism. The sooner you get rid of them the better'.*[71]

Zhirinovsky took Le Pen's tactical advice. The leadership of the LDPR split. On 14 November Arkhipov, Zharikov, Limonov and four other members of the shadow cabinet (only Zhirinovsky himself and two others did not attend) met at a luxury *dacha* (country house) outside Moscow to form the Right-Radical Party. However, the others eventually decided to return to the fold, leaving the 'young men in leather jackets' to fend for themselves, accusing Zhirinovsky of bureaucratism, lack of radicalism and, of course, 'Jewish blood'.[72]

One should be clear that this was no split between supporters and opponents of national socialism. In the first place, Zhirinovsky has never said that he expelled his former colleagues because they are Nazis, but because 'they weren't serious'.[73] On the other hand, Zharikov has stated that 'the Leader [Zhirinovsky] reads Hitler, Himmler and Goebbels in his free time'.[74] Rather the split in the LDPR reflects tactical differences between Nazis throughout Europe over the relationship between the core of stormtroopers and the softer periphery that extends all the way to the passive voter. Zhirinovsky's flexibility has enabled him to scale the heights of Russian politics and to have a real impact on events, standing him in good stead for future crises when the emphasis can shift to the Nazi core, to be used as a battering ram against workers' organisation. He has been careful about advertising his sympathy for Nazism, because he is operating in a country that still remembers 30 million dead as a result of the war with Hitler. It is still early for him to find widespread acceptance for Nazi explanations of the war—ie that Hitler was the victim of a Zionist plot.

But the record of Zhirinovsky's collaboration with people who do not attempt to hide their views is conclusive when considering the existence of a militarised core (the Falcons have not been disbanded) and the mass of circumstantial evidence concerning Zhirinovsky's Nazism: his threats to nuke Japan and the Baltic States, to ban all political parties and strikes and extend Russia's borders to the Indian Ocean, his autobiography which mirrors so much of *Mein Kampf*, his vicious anti-Semitism and so on. All this is quite apart from the obvious delight among activists in other Nazi groups after Zhirinovsky's election success in December 1993—at Moscow State University they gloatingly told anti-Nazi activists, 'We've won!'

Since Zhirinovsky's rise to prominence there have been several reports claiming the LDPR is a puppet of the KGB. The mayor of St Petersburg, Anatoly Sobchak, for example, implicates Gorbachev himself. Leading politicians such as Galina Staravoitova and Alexander Yakovlev have also stated that the KGB formed the LDPR in an attempt to create a pocket opposition when the Communist Party was on the verge of collapse.[75]

These claims do not conflict with the circumstances of Zhirinovsky's political past. Educated at an elite language university and allowed to travel abroad, Zhirinovsky was clearly no stranger to the KGB. His party was the first to be registered after the removal of the one party clause from the Soviet Constitution, and he was immediately granted access to central venues when other opposition parties were still semi-legal. An invitation to Zhirinovsky to join Gorbachev on Lenin's mausoleum in November 1990 for the annual parade to celebrate the revolution is still on display in the Museum of the Revolution just across from the Kremlin.

A party such as the LDPR, claiming to be liberal but against 'democratic excesses' and uncritical of the KGB could clearly have met the requirements of the Soviet state at a critical juncture. Without doubt Zhirinovsky enjoys widespread support in the police and army today. But the LDPR is far from being the obedient tool of the Russian secret services that can be safely wound up should it get out of control. Zhirinovsky's political origins say more about the nature of the Russian state than about the party that he leads.

Barkashov and the blackshirts

Since the events of October 1993 the name of Alexander Petrovich Barkashov has appeared regularly on Russian television and in the national press. In this sense the October attempt 'to take the Kremlin by storm' (Rutskoi's appeal from the White House balcony) played the same role for Barkashov as the Beer-Hall Putsch for Hitler—it shot him to national prominence.

In 1990 Barkashov's Russian National Unity (RNU) organisation split from the main Nazi outfit at the time, *Pamyat* (Memory), which fractured into half a dozen groups at the end of the 1980s.[76] RNU is distinguished from other Nazi groups by its blackshirt uniform and its use of the swastika as 'the symbol of the future Russia'.[77] In October 1993 several dozen of its members played a leading role in the defence of the parliament and shocked Russian public opinion by parading up and down outside the White House wearing swastika armbands and giving Nazi salutes. Barkashov's publications make it clear that Russia awaits the same 'national reawakening' that took place in Germany in 1933, Italy in 1922 and Spain in 1936.[78] RNU propagates a particularly foul brand of anti-Semitism.

Barkashov has achieved what Zhirinovsky and others have yet to accomplish: he has put significant numbers of young men in uniform and set them marching. During the October by-election campaign in a Moscow suburb election meetings attended by all candidates were packed with hundreds of youths in combat gear and swastikas, who drowned their opponents down with shouts of, 'Less people, more oxygen!', and 'Zionism shall not pass'.[79] Barkashov's candidate promised to introduce eugenic birth programmes and to 'exterminate' homosexuals. He won almost 10,000 votes (5.9 percent).

Barkashov's organisation is extensive. According to a high ranking member who turned against the organisation:

> *There are over 10,000 'brothers-in-arms'* [the highest of the three membership levels in RNU, forming the organisation's nucleus] *throughout Russia. In Moscow alone there are over 500 people. There are over half a million 'fellow campaigners' and 'supporters'. But there are also 'sympathisers'—*

> *who can count them all? RNU is slowly but steadily gathering strength. People in the police, army and high-placed ministerial figures are currying favour with RNU... Barkashov's people enjoy particular sympathy among leaders of the National Salvation Front, Labouring Russia, national-bolshevik groups, the nationalist element of the Orthodox priesthood, some deputies to the State Duma and even heads of the administrations of cities and oblasts.*[80]

This may not be an exaggerated assessment (although it is rather too similar to that given by Barkashov himself, and the figure of 10,000 core members doesn't tally with the much lower figure for the capital itself), and its latter half is certainly accurate. This makes RNU the fourth largest political party in Russia after the LDPR. In March 1994 Barkashov established the National Social Movement as a Nazi trade union along with Alexander Alexeyev, leader of the Confederation of Free Trade Unions of Russia, one of the largest independent trade union federations in the country, claiming over 200,000 members. In a joint statement they declared that 'the class struggle between employers and wage workers is a fanatical Marxist-Zionist invention. The interests of employers and workers should not clash'.[81] According to one report, the Nazis have a significant base in the massive Severstal steel plant in Cherepovetsk and have begun to establish contact with Vorkuta miners.[82]

In view of its openly Nazi ideology, why is RNU so successful? Barkashov seems to have grasped that the key to success in mobilising people demoralised and disorientated by the crisis is brute, naked force. His organisation is held in awe by nationalist opponents of the Yeltsin regime, who are spellbound by the uniforms, the muscular young men, their certainty and heroic image. This has enabled Barkashov to reach mutual agreement with General Sterligov's Russian National Assembly, Stanislav Terekhov's Union of Officers and other nationalist organisations and to begin to unite the myriad nationalist groupings. Most significantly, the big Moscow weekly *Zavtra*, edited by Alexander Prokhanov, who sees his role as uniting the various currents on the far right, has become a propaganda organ for Barkashov, gushing praise for the RNU, repeating its sordid lie that Israeli troops led Yeltsin's attack on parliament in October 1993 and so on.

RNU strikes fear into its opponents and makes its uniformed supporters feel that they deserve respect. On a somewhat more prosaic level, one of the latter says that no one asks them to pay when they get on the metro: 'And in the train itself everyone squeezes up and they all sit quietly until you get off'.[83]

The Red-Browns and the Russian Strasserites

There are several umbrella organisations in Russia that bring Nazi, monarchist and extreme nationalist groupings together with supporters of the former regime, people and organisations that call themselves Communist. The best known of these is the National Salvation Front, whose secretary was for a time the leader of the Communist Party of the Russian Federation, Gennady Zyuganov. The front has been responsible for massive demonstrations in Moscow of hundreds of thousands of people, sometimes leading to bloody clashes with the police. Here you can find placards of Stalin rubbing shoulders with the black, white and gold flags of the Romanovs. This phenomenon has become popularly known as the 'Red-Brown' movement, uniting the 'Reds' with the 'Brownshirts'.

Politically these apparently diverse forces are agreed in their demand for an end to democracy, the introduction of a state of emergency (the programme of the August 1991 putschists), an end to military-civil conversion in the arms industry and the resurrection of Russia as a great imperial power.

The ideological cement of the movement is Great Russian nationalism. Take the Communist Party of the Russian Federation (CPRF), for example, an organisation that numbers over half a million members. Gennady Zyuganov's latest book, *Great Power* (1994), claims to set out the central planks of the CPRF's politics. Zyuganov makes no attempt to distinguish nation from class, and offers but one small apology to Marx, who apparently considered his theories to be applicable only to Western Europe, and to Lenin, who apparently argued to unite all classes so as to stand at the head of the nation.[84]

For Zyuganov, Moscow is to become the 'Third Rome', 'Holy *Rus*', destined to fulfill the tsarist trinity of 'autocracy, Orthodoxy and nation'. Russia must fight a 'national liberation struggle' against 'transnational, cosmopolitan forces' of the 'world oligarchy', against 'naked russophobia' and 'crazed persecution of Russian writers', to resurrect the USSR, 'the historical and geopolitical inheritor of the Russian empire'. He talks of returning Russia's 'natural geopolitical borders' to include the 'little Russians' (ie the Ukrainians) and Byelorus. He considers the CPRF to be a party of *derzhavniki* (great power supporters), of 'patriots' who have 'rejected the extremist theses of class struggle' to unite the workers with 'nationally oriented entrepreneurs'.[85] Finally he adds:

> *It is time for us to recognise that the Russian Orthodox Church is the historical foundation and expression of the 'Russian idea' in the form polished by ten centuries of our statehood... The most powerful means of undermining the Russian national consciousness, the main tool for splitting it...are the endless*

attempts to antagonistically juxtapose in people's minds the 'white' and 'red' national ideas... By reuniting the 'red' ideal...with the 'white' ideal...Russia will at last attain its craved-for social, cross-class consensus and imperial might, bequeathed by tens of generations of our ancestors, achieved through the courage and holy suffering of the heroic history of the Fatherland! [86]

From the above it ought to be clear why Zyuganov can happily appear on a platform with Alexander Barkashov. In the autumn of 1994 the CPRF even proposed a new national motto, *Slavyas Rossiya!*—Glory to Russia! This is identical in meaning and but a slight verbal modification on Barkashov's version of *sieg heil*: *Slava Rossii!* pronounced with outstretched arms by his young Nazi thugs. Zyuganov, however, represents the 'moderate' wing of the Communists. Between the CPRF and Barkashov are a number of major organisations laying claim to the Stalinist heritage of the USSR.

First among these is Victor Anpilov and his Russian Communist Workers Party (RCWP). Anpilov is the popular leader of the mass movement Labouring Russia. One of the newspapers claiming to represent the movement—*Chto delat?* (*What Is To Be Done?*)—is edited by the Nazi Vladimir Yakushev, leader of the National-Social Union mentioned above, and is full of anti-Semitic filth. Anpilov popularises a brand of 'Gulag revisionism' which says that Stalin's camps weren't as bad as they are made out to be, and that anyway the end justified the means. According to him, the October revolution swept away the regime that had destroyed the Russian Empire in February.[87] Anpilov is well aware of the history of Stalin's vicious anti-Semitism, and fully approves:

Stalin saw the danger to the party, bled dry by the bitter war, represented by the remnants of the Zionist Bund that had wormed their way into the Bolsheviks in 1917 and quickly seized the key posts in the party and the state. With typical decisiveness Stalin took practical measures to restore the proletarian character of the party.[88]

The Central Committee of the RCWP includes General Albert Makashov, who led Gorbachev's crackdown on the Armenian independence movement in Yerevan in 1987-88. In October 1993 Makashov appeared surrounded by Barkashov's machine gun toting Nazis and led the storming of the Moscow Town Hall.

Another leading figure to advocate 'national bolshevism' (the Russian analogue of German national socialism) is Eduard Limonov.[89] After breaking from Zhirinovsky he has made several attempts to unite 'ultra-communists' with Nazis, the latest being the launch in November 1994 of the National Bolshevik Party. At a talk at Moscow State University to 250 students in November 1994 he called for a ban on individual freedom, the establishment of a network of informers on every block, the creation of a 'Führer regime', and so on.

In June 1994 Limonov united with Barkashov to form the 'National-Revolutionary Movement', which has a red flag with a white circle and a black hammer and sickle.[90] (Hitler's flag was red with a white circle in the middle and a black swastika.) On the pages of *Zavtra* Limonov and Barkashov made an appeal to 'Anpilov, red brother' to join them.[91] Anpilov declined to attend the launch event, but sent his greetings. National bolshevism has attracted some well known supporters. The rock singers Yegor Letov and Pauk (Sergei Troitsky) of the heavy metal groups *Grazhdanskaya Oborona* and *Korroziya Metala* are cult figures among Russian youth. Their packed concerts often include the appearance of uniformed Barkashov supporters giving Nazi salutes on stage, and are inevitably accompanied by the sale of Nazi literature.

Hitler and Mussolini also had 'left wings' that emphasised the 'anti-capitalist' element of this essentially reactionary ideology—in Germany they were associated with leaders of the SA butchered by Hitler during the 'night of the long knives', 30 June 1934. This brought the petty bourgeois radicals to heel after they had done the dirty work of smashing the trade unions and the Communists. Daniel Guerin has described at length how Hitler's Nazis combined their support for capitalism with an anti-capitalist rhetoric:

> *It was Gregor Strasser who became the brilliant and tireless propagandist of this synthesis: 'German industry and economy in the hands of international finance capital means the end of all possibility of social liberation; it means the end of all dreams of a socialist Germany... We National Socialist revolutionaries, we ardent socialists, are waging the fight against capitalism and imperialism... German socialism will be possible and lasting only when Germany is freed!'* [92]

Variations on Strasser's words can be heard at any Red-Brown meeting in Moscow. Limonov makes explicit reference to this side of the ideology of Hitler and Mussolini, and writes: 'At least Hitler was a revolutionary'.[93] Limonov and Anpilov are the Strasserites of the Nazi movement in Russia today.

The roots of Russian nationalism

The strength of the Russian hard right and its rapid rise to prominence are proof of widespread Russian nationalism in the USSR. But the phenomenon continues to baffle many on the left, who saw in the Soviet Union a buffer against nationalism and a bastion of 'friendship of peoples' (to use the hackneyed old Soviet slogan). Thus, in his otherwise useful book on Yeltsin's Russia, the *Guardian's* Jonathan Steele concludes that the emergence of a 'strong Russian national state' is an impossibility, and that 'for the Communists [Russian nationalism] was impossible, given the long tradition of Soviet "internationalism" and the desire to preserve the USSR'.[94] Contrary to such widespread assumptions, however, a central element in Stalin's counter-revolution was the restoration of Russian nationalism to the status of the dominant and at times official ideology. The Soviet Union was undoubtedly the *Russian* empire, staffed by Russians inspired by a messianic Russian nationalism, the great majority of them members of the Communist Party.

None of this should come as any surprise to socialists today:[95] in the last years of his life Lenin was well aware that the bureaucratic degeneration of the workers' state in Russia was opening the floodgates of Russian nationalism. It was precisely on the national question that he first prepared to do battle with the bureaucracy.[96] In 1922 he declared his intention to 'defend the non-Russians from the onslaught of that really Russian man, the Great-Russian chauvinist, in substance a rascal and a tyrant, such as the typical Russian bureaucrat'.[97]

Already in 1922 Stalin was accusing Lenin of 'national-liberalism'. 'They [the bureaucrats] say we need a united apparatus', Lenin replied, 'but where did these assurances come from? Did they not come from that same Russian apparatus which we took over from tsarism and only slightly annointed with Soviet oil?' Lenin was preparing to give battle to 'the Great-Russian chauvinist riffraff' at the Twelfth Party Congress in the spring of 1923, but illness prevented him.[98]

Throughout the 1920s Russian nationalist tendencies in the state, literature and art grew in intensity, as Agursky shows in some detail.[99] But a *qualitative* shift occurred in the first half of the 1930s. According to the emigre sociologist Nikolai Timasheff, this was one of the most striking elements of Stalin's 'Great Retreat' from the original aims of the revolution: 'in 1934...the trend suddenly changed, giving place to one of the most conspicuous phases of the Great Retreat, which in the course of a few years transformed Russia into a country with much more fervent nationalism than she ever had before the attempt of international transfiguration'.[100]

As John Dunlop notes in his studies of contemporary Russian nationalism, Russian nationalists today also recognise the significance of the dramatic reversal in official attitudes to Russian nationalism at this time.[101] As the officially sponsored Russian nationalist journal *Molodaya Gvardiya* put it in 1970:

> *A nihilistic raging in respect to the cultural achievements of our past was unfortunately rather fashionable among a segment of our intelligentsia in the 20s... Pokrovsky and his 'school' placed a fat minus sign before the entire history of Russia... In his* [Pokrovsky's] *essays on Russian history (which it would be more correct to term essays on anti-Russian history) the names of* [the tsarist generals] *Suvorov and Kutuzov are virtually not mentioned... Now it is clear that in the task of the struggle with the destroyers and nihilists the break occurred in the middle of the 30s.*[102]

From the mid-30s onwards Russian history reappeared as a sequence of magnificent deeds performed by Russia's national heroes—the princes of Kiev, the tsars of Moscow, the dignitaries of the church, the generals and admirals of the empire. Symbols of Russian medieval barbarism such as Peter the Great entered the gallery of national heroes. In 1938 Eisenstein's film *Alexander Nevsky*, celebrating the life of this medieval prince, was shown on the eve of the anniversary of the revolution. Then came the turn of generals of Catherine the Great and Alexander I: Suvorov was honoured in a film and Kutuzov glorified in a book by the historian Tarle, welcomed back from emigration. Later still came the positive re-evaluation of Prince Bagration, who defeated Napoleon at the battle of Borodino, 'rehabilitation' for the leaders of Russia's First World War campaigns, and in the early 1940s Alexei Tolstoy, the most acclaimed Russian author of the time, was given the honour of writing a play to glorify Ivan the Terrible (Eisenstein's film was first shown in 1944). The study of Russian history was reintroduced to the school curriculum, creating major problems since there was no patriotic school textbook available.[103]

Russian nationalism reached its apogee during the war. In the words of Alexander Solzhenitsyn, whose political views are on the far right of the spectrum:

> *From the very first days of the war Stalin refused to rely on the putrid decaying prop of ideology. He wisely discarded it and unfurled instead the old Russian banner—sometimes, indeed, the standards of Orthodoxy—and we conquered!*[104]

Glorification of Russian history played a major role in mobilising the war effort. In 1941 anti-religious organisations and publications were closed down and the Orthodox church was rehabilitated. Tsarist uniforms and epaulettes were restored in the army in 1943. Elite military schools were named after Suvorov, Kutuzov and Nakhimov. On 1 January 1944 the *Internationale*, the USSR's national anthem since 1918, was replaced by a new nationalist hymn with the opening line, 'The unbreakable union of free republics has been forged through the

Great *Rus*'. At the end of the war Stalin pronounced his famous toast: 'To the health of the Russian people!'[105]

The post-war years until Stalin's death saw a fearsome nationalist campaign led by Zhdanov, cracking down on 'rootless cosmopolitanism' in culture and the arts. Almost all the wars waged by tsarist Russia were proclaimed just and progressive, including the expansionist policies of the pre-revolutionary empire. Classical Russian opera was officially proclaimed 'the best in the world', and all Western art from the Impressionists onwards classified as 'decadent'. Over many years the Soviet press published systematic claims that Russians were leaders in all fields: it wasn't Edison who invented the electric light, but Lodygin; the Cherepanovs built a steam engine before Stephenson; the telegraph was in use in Russia before Morse in America; Chernov invented steel; even penicillin was announced a Russian discovery. Everything from the bicycle to the aeroplane was declared to be the fruit of Russian talent.[106]

No wonder that today's Russian nationalists remember the Stalin period with such fondness! For Zyuganov, leader of the Communist Party, given a few more years Stalin could have effected a total reversal to the pre-revolution period:

> *If its momentum had been maintained, this 'ideological* ***perestroika****' would have left no doubt that in 10 to 15 years the USSR would have fully overcome the negative spiritual consequences of the revolutionary upheavals... Stalin needed just five or seven more years to make his 'ideological perestroika' irreversible and secure the resurrection of the unjustifiably interrupted traditions of Russian spirit and statehood.*[107]

The post-Stalin period saw many of these tendencies criticised and somewhat softened under pressure from below, but Russian nationalism remained a key prop of the regime, which continued to direct its ire mainly at the nationalism of the non-Russian republics. The consequences of post-Stalin Russification and national oppression have been described elsewhere in this journal.[108] But in understanding the strength of Russian nationalism today it is important to grasp that Stalin's legacy in this area was barely scratched, and on the contrary flourished under Khrushchev, Brezhnev and their successors.

Indeed, Russian nationalism was used to combat the democratic 'excesses' brought on by the Khrushchev thaw and the Prague Spring. As described in detail by Yanov and Dunlop, the 1960s and 1970s saw a constant tension within the Soviet leadership over the extent to which Russian nationalists should be given a free hand.[109] In the 1960s nationalists 'were free to an astonishing degree to air their views in the official press'.[110] Nationalists took control of leading journals such as *Molodaya*

Gvardiya, published by the Central Committee of the Komsomol which was but one of the many mass circulation publications to come under nationalist control. Nationalist dissidents received much more lenient treatment than those such as Andrei Sakharov, exiled to Gorky, who criticised the regime from the point of view of Western liberal democracy.[111] The appalling Russian chauvinist and anti-Semitic paintings by Ilya Glazunov, for example, earned him major exhibitions in Moscow and Leningrad in 1978 and one of the finest *dachas* (country homes) of the Brezhnev period.[112] The strength of the Soviet Writers Union as a bastion of Russian chauvinism under *perestroika* is an indication of the extent to which nationalist writers were encouraged—their books were produced in print runs of hundreds of thousands (many figures in the Soviet Writers Union are now leading Nazi ideologists, such as Prokhanov and Bondarenko). Throughout the 1970s these and other writers made increasing attempts to weld a common ideology integrating the Communist period into the credo of the nationalist right. When Alexander Yakovlev, head of the Central Committee's propaganda department, came out with criticism of brute Russian nationalism in the early 1970s he was swiftly demoted and packed off to Canada as a diplomat.[113]

Surveying this history back in 1986, Yanov concluded that the maintainance of a strong 'dissident right' in the Soviet Union was a conscious decision by the leadership to retain a fallback option to the establishment ideology. The official 'Communist' right understood that the growing crisis of the Soviet system demanded counter-reform. According to this logic:

> *reform demands a radical change in ideology capable of restoring the empire's former mobilisational character, securing the active co-operation and support of the masses and parts of the intelligentsia, and of justifying a sharp increase in production, family and cultural discipline and a resurrection of a fighting expansionist dynamic. Orthodox Marxism is no longer capable of such a shift. It cannot justify a return to the ideological atmosphere of war communism* [1918-21]... *In other words, counter-reform demands an ideological strategy, for the development of which the 'establishment right' has no intellectual or moral resources apart from those that inspire its hounded and persecuted dissident sister. In this sense it is certainly intellectually 'vulnerable' to the more precise dissident nationalists.*[114]

It would be wrong, however, to see Russian nationalism as merely a bureaucratic conspiracy to keep the masses down. Russian nationalism was deeply ingrained in the Soviet Russian population, just as in any other capitalist nation state under normal conditions. By its very nature, the totalitarian dictatorship precluded detailed sociological research, attitude surveys and so on. But there are certain useful indicators of the strength of Russian nationalism in the population, such as letters to the *samizdat* (unofficial) journal *Veche*, the mass membership of organisations involved in restoring national monuments, and of course the stunning popularity of artists such as Glazunov.[115] In a society in which workers have been defeated, atomised, their organisations crushed, we would expect nationalist ideas to find a fertile ground.

Anti-Semitism

If Stalin was prepared to use Russian nationalism to cement a social base for his regime, he certainly had no scruples about restoring anti-Semitism to official status. Though the revolution had staunched the wounds of anti-Jewish feeling in the population, enabling Jews such as Trotsky, Zinoviev and Sverdlov to become national figures, the revolution's defeat saw the gangrene grip the patient harder than ever. When Shulgin, the tsarist politician whose anti-Semitic tirades plumb the very depths, made a secret visit to Russia in 1926, he was delighted to find widespread anti-Semitism:

> *I thought I was going to a dead country, but I saw the awakening of a great country... The Communists will give power to the fascists...* [Russia] *has eliminated the dreadful socialist rubbish in the course of just a few years. Of course, they'll soon liquidate the Yids.*[116]

Stalin's war on Trotsky and the Left Opposition was carried out under the banner of anti-Semitism. As Trotsky later wrote:

> *After Zinoviev and Kamenev came over to the opposition the situation rapidly worsened. Now there was an excellent opportunity to tell the workers that the opposition is led by 'three disgruntled Jewish intellectuals'. At Stalin's command Uglanov in Moscow and Kirov in Leningrad followed this line systematically and almost completely openly... Not only in the countryside but even in Moscow factories baiting of the opposition by 1926 often took an absolutely clear anti-Semitic character. Many agitators openly said: 'The Yids are playing up'. I received hundreds of letters complaining about anti-Semitic methods in the struggle against the Opposition.*[117]

From Germany Hitler's companions Ribbentrop, Strasser and Goebels observed this process with glee—Strasser was convinced that Stalin's aim was to stop the revolution and liquidate communism.[118]

The purges of the mid-1930s meant a further turn for the worse, with organised Jewish life almost completely paralysed: Jewish schools were closed in their hundreds along with Jewish newspapers and departments of Yiddish language and culture. During the years of the Nazi-Soviet pact (1939-41) the Soviet press ceased to report on Nazi persecution of the Jews and the murder of Jews in Poland after war broke out.[119]

The post-war period saw another flare-up of anti-Semitism in Russia, linked—as with Zhdanov's nationalist campaign—to the need to re-establish strict control after the upheaval of war. In 1948 arrests began of the Anti-Fascist Committee, run by the director of the Jewish State Theatre in Moscow, Solomon Mikhoels, who was accused of leading a 'pro-American Zionist conspiracy'. His arrest and murder were followed by the roundup and murder of the Jewish intelligentsia. A book on Nazi crimes against the Jews was banned and its authors were prevented from defending themselves. In 1953 the campaign reached fever-pitch with the 'discovery' of the 'Doctor's plot', the alleged conspiracy of nine doctors, six of them Jews, to murder the Soviet leadership. All Jews came under suspicion and thousands were dismissed from their jobs. Only Stalin's death may have prevented plans to deport the Jewish population to Siberia, just like the Balts, Poles, Tatars and Caucasus peoples before and during the war. Khrushchev told the author Ilya Ehrenburg of a conversation with Stalin in which the latter voiced this intention. There is evidence that cattle trucks were prepared in 1953 and that lists of victims were drawn up.[120]

In the post-Stalin period anti-Semitism flourished under the banner of 'anti-Zionism', an official campaign of a mass character after the Six Day War of 1967. The ideas were extremely crude. From the late 1960s onwards every year dozens of books and hundreds of articles were published relentlessly spreading the same message: namely that the idea of Judaism is the idea of world fascism, the Old Testament was fascist, so were Moses, King Solomon and almost all other Jewish leaders; the Jews had always been aggressors and mass murderers, parasites taught to destroy and subjugate other peoples with the aim of world domination; the Jews had been the pioneers of capitalism; they were in the forefront of anti-Communism and nurtured a burning hatred of Russian culture; Hitler and other Nazis had been mere puppets in their hands, inciting them to make war against the USSR in 1941; they had connived with Hitler to persecute German Jews—in far fewer numbers than claimed by Jews themselves—with the aim of establishing a Jewish state in Israel; and so on and so forth. Hundreds of thousands of copies of pulp fiction were pumped out by the armed forces publishing house featuring lurid tales of ritual Jewish murders and plots.[121] As Lacquer comments, 'By the early 1980s it was legitimate to argue that there had never been anti-

Jewish pogroms in tsarist Russia, but merely legitimate acts of self-defence against Jewish provocations.'[122]

In sum, it has been necessary to dwell on the history of Soviet Russian nationalism and anti-Semitism at some length because it is totally ignored or played down by the left in Britain and elsewhere. Some 60 years of Stalinism have provided fertile soil for the rise of the Russian Nazis today. Only gross complacency or political paralysis can allow Jonathan Steele, for example, to talk about 'nationalism at a low level' in Yeltsin's Russia, as if this was the heritage of some glorious Soviet internationalism.[123] On the contrary, the Soviet dictatorship was vicious in every respect. Small wonder that Konstantin Rodzayevsky, leader of the Russian Fascist Party in exile in China after the war, could write, 'Stalinism is exactly what we mistakenly called "Russian fascism". It is our Russian fascism cleansed of extremes, illusions and errors.'[124]

Why no social democracy?

The phenomenon of the Red-Browns, a mass movement of extreme nationalists led by the Communist Party, is unique to post-*perestroika* Eastern Europe. Why should Russia have taken a different path, and what does this say about the potential for the hard right to grow?

Elsewhere the collapse of Communism has seen a rapid transformation of the Communist Parties along the lines of Western parliamentary socialist, social democratic parties: in September 1993 the Social Democratic Party of Poland formed the Left Democratic Alliance with the Peasant Party and won the elections; in Hungary in June 1994 the Socialist Party came to power, followed by the Bulgarian Socialist Party in November; in East Germany the Party of Democratic Socialism has 30 percent support in some towns. These are Tony Blair style parties that reject most of their Communist past, preach the market and claim to offer privatisation 'with a human face'. The Social Democratic Party in Poland has a real base in the former official trade unions, and can therefore be considered a social democratic party in more than name only.

There have been several attempts to do the same in Russia, all of which have flopped. In June 1990 Boris Kagarlitsky led an initiative to found a Socialist Party. When this effort petered out 18 months later, a few anarchists and an official trade union leader were roped in to form a Party of Labour (PL)—modelled on the British Labour Party[125]—and standing for 'the rights of consumers and independent national entrepreneurs; for a civilised market; for inclusion in the world economy to secure the development of the national economy; for honest government in the framework of a mixed economy'.[126] In the newspaper of the official trade unions Kagarlitsky wrote, 'We not only can but must create conditions for the growth of independent private business "from below", defending it from being crushed by the monopolies and from failure in conditions of economic chaos.'[127]

The PL never managed to gain more than a tiny handful of members—though its young anarchist members allowed the official trade unions to put on a left face for a while.

After the August 1991 coup, the historian Roy Medvedyev was instrumental in forming the Socialist Party of Labourers, which initially claimed some 60,000 members. However, with the resurrection of the Communist Party many of Medvedyev's members drifted back to the fold. The attempt in 1990 by the young economist Oleg Rumyantsev to form a Social Democratic Party also got little further than a launch conference and a few programmatic documents. Rumyantsev later became one of Rutskoi's supporters and is known for his hard nationalist views.

In 1994 there were two further attempts to form a social democratic party 'from above'. In July Gavriil Popov, the wily old ex-mayor of Moscow, attended the Congress of the Independent Miners Union and returned calling for a 'united front of parties and movements representing the interests of the non-bureaucratic classes'.[128] In September he got together with other well known representatives of 'non-bureaucratic classes'—such as Alexander Yakovlev (formerly Communist Party Central Committee member) and Yevgeny Shaposhnikov (formerly minister of defence and now a member of the board of Russia's monopoly arms exporter)—to form the 'United Movement of Social Democrats'.[129] Yakovlev called for 'reform with a human face', while Shaposhnikov announced that 'we never had any real socialism', but 'a devilish mix of state capitalism, totalitarianism and dogmatism'.[130]

This initiative was swiftly followed by another. In October the founding conference of the Russian Social-Democratic Union took place in a hotel in Moscow. The array of 'non-bureaucrats' at this gathering was only slightly less impressive than that of its competitor: Vasily Lipitsky, vice-chairman of Rutskoi's party and none other than Mikhail Gorbachev, who used the occasion to attempt a return to politics. Also involved were the Party of Labour, the Green Party, a leader of the Moscow official trade unions and a number of independent unions. The conference roundly attacked the 'United Movement of Social Democrats' and (shamelessly) accused them of a *Gaponshchina*, a reference to Father Gapon, who was used by the regime in tsarist times to set up a puppet workers' movement under the control of the secret police.[131]

Why should such seasoned defenders of the status quo be seeking to form a social democratic organisation? They clearly care little for workers' interests. However, three years of shock therapy have destroyed

Russians' faith in Yeltsin and the Democrats. On the other hand, the Communist Party is still deeply disliked by the population. Finally, the success of 'reformed Communists' in Eastern Europe suggests an opportunity to fill a political vacuum in Russia and seize the initiative from the Nazis, who undoubtedly represent a threat to reform orientated sections of the ruling class. Gorbachev, Popov and so on want workers' growing discontent with the system to be directed into safer channels. The Moscow intellectual Sergei Karaganov sums up this attitude:

> *I don't believe in the socialist idea, not even in an enlightened variant, and I consider...individual freedom, private initiative and the ideas of liberalism to be more effective. I don't want a victory for the new social democratic bloc. But I would welcome its appearance.*[132]

But these latest initiatives are doomed to go the way of their predecessors. In the first place, the creation of a mass base for a social democratic party as a buffer between capital and labour demands a general level of working class consciousness and organisation, themselves a product of prolonged and large scale class struggle. The British Labour Party is a good example, as more recently are the Workers Party in Brazil, the ANC in South Africa and the Portuguese Socialist Party. But workers' struggle in Russia since *perestroika* has not come anywhere near such peaks of militancy.

The eruption of struggle around the miners' strike in 1989 influenced the setting up of left organisations such as the Socialist Party and gave birth to new unions, such as the Independent Miners Union and Sotsprof. But the expected resurgence of militancy never came. Prime minister Ryzhkov backed off from price rises in the summer of 1990, and neither the miners' strike of spring 1991 nor the ten day workers' revolt in Minsk that March served to spark a new explosion. The result was a disorientation amongst the emerging left, still bearing the scars of Stalinism, and a rapid bureaucratisation and corruption of the new independent unions.

The leadership of the Independent Miners Union, for example, was split open by financial scandal, and one of its leaders even announced that prioritising workers' collective interests over personal ones was 'a hangover from totalitarianism'. The union's Congress in December 1991 was attended by the British scab 'union', the UDM.[133] Sotsprof has a Moscow membership of several thousands, has supported strikes and encountered hostility from the government for opposing its no-strike rule in 'essential' sectors of the economy. But Sotsprof's leadership is pro-privatisation and eventually backed down on the no-strike clause in return for official recognition. Other independent union groupings such as the Confederation of Labour have suffered decline.

In contrast, the official unions remained relatively intact. The Moscow Federation of Trade Unions, for example, has over 5 million subs paying members. At the end of 1990 the official unions renamed themselves the Federation of Independent Trade Unions of Russia and took steps to distance themselves from the state. One of the most radical steps was the employment by the Moscow leadership of young anarcho-syndicalists to produce the union's newspaper, *SolidArity*.

Andrei Isaev, a leading figure in the Confederation of Anarcho-Syndicalists and for a time the paper's editor, explained why he threw in his lot with the anarchists' old foes. For the first years of *perestroika* he fought for a union like *Solidarnosc* in Poland. But six years went by and no *Solidarnosc* appeared. And indeed, the spontaneous movement put forward peculiar demands: *for* privatisation, *for* individual employment contracts, *for* the market. Then last year the miners struck in support of Yeltsin and their new union was rocked by corruption. The independent unions seemed to be a flop. And finally, despite the collapse of the old Communist Party and its other attendant institutions, the official trade unions were still in one piece with a large infrastructure embracing 99 percent of all workplaces.[134] Therefore Andrei and his young comrades joined with the Moscow official unions and involved themselves in failed attempts to set up a Party of Labour.

In the absence of a break through in the class struggle the logic of their position was to look to the Communist Party as the potential membership for a political party of the unions, as in Eastern Europe. Kagarlitsky made it clear that the PL's eyes were firmly on the Communist Party:

> *Our main cadres could come from the old structures... In this case people will bring with them their old* ***apparat*** *customs, style of work and prejudices. But the unity of unofficial activists with ex Communist Party members will create the best opportunities for the development of a modern left party.*[135]

Why didn't the PL succeed in this intention? The Communist Party's success after it was banned during the August 1991 coup was indeed phenomenal. Within a few months Zyuganov could rightly claim to be leader of the biggest party in Russia, with over half a million members. The party spawned several splits such as Anpilov's Russian Communist Workers Party and Nina Andreyeva's All-Union Communist Party of Bolsheviks, both noted for their Stalin worship. Each of these small organisations were far bigger, vocal and active than all the 'social democrats' put together.

But, unlike its counterparts in Eastern Europe, the Russian Communist Party is structurally far more immune to change. Russia was the centre of empire and therefore the centre of reaction, and the Communist Party was the organiser of this reaction. Its roots go far deeper into society than elsewhere: it is older, more cut off from outside influences, and its control of the economy more total and all embracing than in the East European satellites. Thus attempts to reform the party and the state bureaucracy have been far more prolonged and crisis prone in Russia, which was the first to start *perestroika* but the last to finish it.[136] The Russian Communist Party has therefore maintained its reactionary politics with few concessions to the changing circumstances: indeed, it has adopted a position on the extreme right of the political spectrum and has extended a hand to the Nazis.

Could the Communist Party under different conditions—the pressure of a massive strike wave, for example—'do an Eastern Europe', start talking left, try to take a lead and represent workers' interests? The answer must be an emphatic no. The party has organised links with neither the independent nor the official trade unions, and it has made no particular efforts in this direction. Nor is there any working class content to its politics, which centre on the notion of national unity. The party's core membership is the layer of minor bureaucrats and officials who lost everything with the collapse of Communism: the leadership is also made up of middle ranking Soviet officials, with few figures from the ruling class of big industrialists and politburo members (Yegor Ligachev being the exception that proves the rule).[137] The party membership is almost all middle aged, a consequence of Brezhnev's 'stagnation', during which there were few shake ups of the apparatus and the bureaucracy aged significantly.

In sum, the Communist Party—and this is even more true of Anpilov's organisation—is the party of the petty bureaucrat. All this does not mean to say that it is beyond opportunistic support for strikes in its struggle for power. But the party's condemnation of miners' strikes in 1993-1994 (because of the latter's support for Yeltsin in 1991) is a taste of things to come. In the 1930s the Soviet Communist Party smashed the working class to smithereens—if necessary its Russian descendant would do the same.

Perspectives

After the August 1991 coup attempt *Socialist Review* made the following remarks concerning the future of Russian politics:

> *There is no way of returning to the command economy. That came to a full stop.* [But] *the rulers find themselves in a cul-de-sac. They can't go forward*

and they can't go back. To achieve a real market economy would mean a massive amount of unemployment. [So] *the ruling class is split in all sorts of ways which are always shifting. Why the coup happened is that there was not a balance of power but a balance of powerlessness. The coup was a contest between two forces that are very weak...*

The conditions for another coup will be there as long as the general crisis continues and as long as there's a hierarchy in the army and the KGB. The eye of the storm—who initiates the crackdown—can be different next time. The workers will learn quite a lot from the defeat of this coup. They will learn that workers can remove conspirators. But those people who backed the coup can learn quite a lot too. They can learn for example, as in Chile, that the next coup must be more ruthless and bloody.

The coup in the USSR was the thin end of the wedge—and this leaves two possibilities. It can become thicker or it can disappear... The problems of the economy remain. Empty stomachs can lead to rebellion or they can lead to submission. And mostly it depends on how long the stomachs have been empty. If it goes on far too long the anger can turn to despair. Millions of unemployed people in Germany joined the Nazis because they were hungry...[138]

The economic cul-de-sac is as much a reality today. In the words of *Finansoviye Izvestiya* of 20 December 1994:

The depression that the Russian economy has slid into after four years of crisis is rapidly destroying both the state sector and the alternative market structures in the productive, financial, trade and insurance spheres. For the present this slump holds no preconditions of recovery. The rate of profit excludes investment in material production in the foreseeable future. The leadership doesn't know what to do next and limits itself to day-to-day management, trying to return control with the help of military, command-administrative and openly police methods.

There can be no end to this state of permanent crisis without a large scale social crisis.

The 'balance of powerlessness' is still a key feature of Russian politics, leading to shifting splits and alliances in the ruling class—rearranging the deckchairs on board the *Titanic*. Whereas in 1991 the ruling class was split along fairly discernable lines, this is not the case today. Earlier there were roughly three groupings: those in favour of retaining the old system more or less intact, the 'market Stalinists' or 'Pinochet marketeers' arguing for China type market reform without democracy, and the backers of Western economic and political liberalism.[139] Now a third dimension—the attitude to imperial decline—has further muddied the political waters. The last three years have seen spectacular shifts among the ruling class, pitting the defenders of the White House in 1991 against each other (Rutskoi, Khasbulatov and Sterligov led the 1993 coup), and bringing the bitter opponents of October 1993 back together in the same camp (Khasbulatov's role as Moscow's puppet in the run up to the Chechen crisis).

A key player—the army—is still relatively weak. Whilst it looked in October 1993 as if the army was coming into its own, able to demand an extension of the state of emergency and hold Moscow in its violent grip for a fortnight, the war in Chechnya has exposed the deep divisions among the generals and the strength of the Afghan syndrome among Russians at large: opinion polls consistently showed 65 to 70 percent opposition to the war. Despite General Lebed's statement in July 1994 that Pinochet had the right idea,[140] there is no figure capable of uniting the army around such a programme. But the fact that the army is seeking such a figure is clear: in December 1993 36 percent of officers, 80 percent of warrant officers, 65 percent of conscripts and 35 percent of Moscow generals voted for Zhirinovsky.[141] But if Zhirinovsky won an election tomorrow he would have to rely on an army demoralised and morally defeated. Desertion of the rank and file and insubordination of high ranking officers were a feature of the Chechen campaign.

Nor is there yet an individual or platform capable of giving vigour and confidence to a major section of the ruling class. The Democrats are weak and leaderless, and are in any case seen as mainly responsible for the crisis. However, the extreme right is still fragmented. There have been umpteen attempts to unite the nationalists into a broad anti-Yeltsin coalition, among which the main events were the founding in February 1992 of the Congress of Civic and Patriotic Forces, the creation of the National Salvation Front in October that same year, and Rutskoi's spring 1994 initiative, Consensus in the Name of Russia. All these organisations have split and split again. The opposition has tried with increasing desperation to find a single acceptable figure to stand for president in 1996, but to no avail, candidates for the post including Rutskoi, the Siberian boss Pyotr Romanov, Yuri Skokov and others. But the 'second rank' of ambitious pretenders to the nationalist throne is broad and deep, and personal frictions have obstructed unity. Zhirinovsky has always been kept at a distance by other Red-Brown leaders, mainly because of his unbridled individual ambition. Furthermore, the peculiar contradictions of Russian nationalism—attitudes to the Soviet period and Russia's historically multinational statehood—have complicated consensus around a common ideology.

Until the state can muster its forces for a decisive crackdown, there will continue to be coup attempts, but they will probably be just as bungled and feeble as the previous ones. The weakness of the ruling class as a whole is one of the reasons why Yeltsin has tottered without falling for so long—there is no one capable of giving him the necessary shove.

It is here that the Nazis can offer the ruling class a helping hand by welding sections of middle class youth and the army to a fanatical dogma that brooks no criticism. Parliament's experiment with Barkashov's Nazis during the October 1993 fighting confirms that sections of the ruling class will increasingly gravitate to extreme solutions. Barkashov was charged with security of the White House and issued with machine guns.[142] He is probably correct in his claim that with twice the number of Nazi stormtroopers he could have marshalled an attack on the Kremlin and shifted the balance in the army against Yeltsin. Even a small band of highly organised and fanatical armed youth can make a decisive difference when opposing forces which are weak and badly organised. This is the Nazis' main strength in Russia at present. During the Chechen crisis the government has come to increasingly rely on Zhirinovsky's voting bloc in the Duma, enabling it to fend off criticism and avoid a no confidence vote.

However, there are also broader horizons for the Russian Nazis. Zhirinovsky, for example, has won a following among some businessmen, such as Sergei Mavrodi, whose 'pyramid' investment scheme robbed thousands of Russians of their savings and made him a rich man, but brought him up against the state, which briefly imprisoned him. People like this may look to the Nazis to take power. A liberal journalist has summed up the thinking of those such as Mavrodi and those in the ruling class who are looking ahead:

> *It cannot be ruled out that the combination of the patriotic idea in a particularly extreme form with a recognition of the values of the free market can be more successful than the compilation of Communism and flabby patriotism currently practised by the large majority of the opposition. It is no accident that Prokhanov, who has done more than anyone to unite the opposition, has recently given more and more space in his paper* **Zavtra** *to representatives of this 'new' opposition. Furthermore, given the growing distrust towards the active political establishment, little-known politicians could turn out to be a good bet, confirmation of which is the electoral history of Zhirinovsky.*[143]

As in Western Europe, the Russian Nazis are still far bigger in electoral terms than on the ground. Although Prokhanov's *Zavtra* is on sale daily in practically every Moscow metro station, the sellers are all elderly: one rarely comes across the young Nazi thugs. Neither Zhirinovsky nor Barkashov has yet organised street demonstrations separately from the big Red-Brown events. The only known instance of a

Nazi demo occurred in spring 1994 after the insurrection in Bophuthatswana, when 50 or so Nazis from Limonov's group appeared in combat fatigues and swastikas outside the South African embassy. One of the few instances of a pogrom reported in the press—which is highly sensitised to the Nazis—occurred in early 1994 when members of the Black Hundreds (the name is that of the main organisation that led pogroms from 1905 to 1917) attacked worshippers at an Orthodox church, followers of Alexander Men, a priest of Jewish origin.

The Nazis are ridden with divisions, just like the rest of the right. The Russian Nazis have a bloody history of internal struggles. In November 1993 Barkashov was shot in the leg from a passing unmarked car. A year later his second in command was knocked down and killed in a hit and run attack in similar circumstances. In December 1994 after the leadership of the National Republican Party of Russia was overturned at its congress, the new leader and his bodyguards were machine gunned down in broad daylight the following day. At the ideological level there is still considerable disagreement—even within Barkashov's organisation—over the use of the swastika in open propaganda. After its poor by-election showing in October, a split opened up in the leadership over Barkashov's tactical shift towards gaining electoral respectability.

On the other hand, there is widespread 'soft' Nazism in Russian society. When selling anti-Nazi literature to students, although the response is generally good, one is struck by the frequency of the reply, 'No thanks, I'm a Nazi.' It is even chic to be Nazi in Russia today, and some young kids and students have little hesitation in describing themselves as such. Despite their own liberal and even left wing views several women acquaintances of mine have Nazi boyfriends. More seriously, the wars in Yugoslavia and the former Soviet republics have provided excellent training grounds for the Nazis. As the journalist Vachnadze puts it:

> *We can't get away from our 9 million young and middle aged people who are experts with weapons and are used to putting them to use. The Gulag, Afghanistan, the Caucasus wars, Moldova and also the criminal amalgam between the militia and the small shopkeepers has provided us with a surplus of killers, adventurists and simply scum.*[144]

In short, there is nothing inherent in Russian society today that rules out the growth of a Nazi mass movement. While the state zigzags from more to less intervention and back, from more to less pressure on the working class, the scale of political discontent is to an extent contained. But the crisis in Russia is huge and unstable. Unexpected events caused by miscalculations or unforeseen events—wars, a run of bankruptcies, a sharp increase in unemployment, loss of state control—can plunge the country into social strife. On the other hand, failure to stop the decline can push the ruling class to try desperate measures with similar consequences.

In such conditions the Nazis could cease to be racist electoral machines or power brokers in ruling class faction fights and make a bid for power, although there is no certainty that Zhirinovsky or Barkashov themselves would front such a movement, and the leader may still be relatively unknown. The idea that some 'enlightened' government will come along to put a stop to them is clearly nonsense, while the outlines of the crisis given above suggest that in certain conditions a right wing mass movement could find significant support within the state and in certain sections of society as a whole. It surely requires more than a dash of complacency to ignore the parallels with late 1920s Germany.

One simple fact, however, cuts through the unpleasantness of this situation. The Russian Nazis have built once already, and fallen apart. At its height *Pamyat* had hundreds, maybe thousands, of members. But in 1989-1990 it fell to pieces, splintering into eight or more tiny groups.[145] This coincided with the peak of radicalisation in the movement for '*glasnost* (openness) from below', when strikes were widespread and militant and the miners' struggle was in full swing. Massive demonstrations took place in Moscow against the invasions of Baku and the Baltic States.

A revival of this movement can forge *class* unity between workers, overcome national divisions and blow the Nazis apart once again.

What about the workers?

There is popular misconception, fed by superficial reports in the press, that Russian workers have become somehow declassed, reduced to selling their personal belongings on street corners in order to make ends meet, uninterested in politics or uncritical of Yeltsin, while Russian society has spiralled down into an abyss of gangsterism, pornography and crime. The real situation is more complex and dynamic than this.

In any capitalist crisis the weak get hit hardest. Pensioners, the unemployed, students, refugees, the chronically sick and disabled are in a frightful situation, as are those living on a single income. It is almost exclusively the elderly who line the major railway stations and exits from the metro to resell bread and milk to hurrying commuters. Violent crime affects mainly the 'new Russians' who have done well out of the market or have jobs with Western firms. Moscow is a lot safer to live in than many Western capitals: as a rough indication, in 1992 the number of crimes committed per 100,000 people was 1,856 in Russia, 5,820 in the USA, 6,169 in France and 7,956 in Britain.[146] Russian cities do not yet have ghettos or deprived inner city areas as in the West.

Two strike waves since 1991 have kept workers' heads above water, the first in the spring of 1992 and the second from November 1993 to the spring of 1994. The weakness of the ruling class has made it susceptible to pressure from below—the danger of provoking a 'social explosion' has been a constant theme in the leadership's battle of words. The 1993-1994 strike wave was significantly more militant than previous ones. It began in November in the Siberian gas town of Nadym. Some 18,000 workers from 72 factories struck for two weeks, blocked all roads into the town, threatened to turn off the pipeline supplying the rest of Russia, and forced the government to agree to pay wages due since the summer. This was followed by a massive one-day strike by half a million miners on 6 December, which continued for five days in Vorkuta winning across the board concessions over wages and redundancy guarantees. There was then a brief lull, punctuated by a strike of meteorological workers at the end of the year. The government refused to honour its promises. This provoked a wave of hunger strikes in the pits in January and February throughout all the mining areas in the country. Several hundred Vorkuta miners refused to come up after the shift on 9 February. The president of the Independent Miners Union described hunger strikes as taking on 'a mass character'. On 10 February communication workers struck for a day, closing down TV and radio broadcasts in 60 cities. On 15 February 164 higher education institutes came out on strikes of up to one day, with large rallies in many towns. On 1 March Moscow ambulance workers came out on indefinite strike and hundreds of thousands of miners struck for several days. This was followed by mass pickets of the White House by miners, teachers and students, defence workers, striking textile workers and fishermen. The threat of renewed strike action in April forced the government to concede to the miners once again. Oil workers and airline pilots also took strike action.

A feature of previous strike waves was that management backed strikes in order to pressure government for subsidies. But now because the state has gradually retreated from the economy, and granted more responsibility to local management, the strikes are marked by greater class polarisation, with management hostility and victimisation of activists. Many strikers also put forward political demands for new elections and the resignation of the government, though there have been no calls to save aspects of the welfare state, which has been utterly decimated. The strikes were defensive and somewhat desperate, as shown by the level of hunger strikes, and without anything like the same optimism and radicalisation of 1989-1990. Most workers have no positive vision of what to fight for, apart from their wages. Whilst privatisation of the pits was a popular demand of strikers in 1991-1992, this is no longer the case. In October 1994 the first strike demanding renationalisation took place in a small factory in the Urals, and was followed by a strike with the same demand of miners in a private pit outside Moscow.

In the face of such struggles it is clearly a problem for Zhirinovsky and Barkashov to argue to ban strikes because they are a Marxist-Zionist invention! The Russian working class is bruised but not broken. This is a hurdle that the Nazis have yet to face. It is one thing to pose in uniform and go to weight training classes, but another altogether to take on one of the largest, best educated and most highly concentrated industrial working classes in the world.

The experience of the last three years has taught Russian workers a lot. The example of Positron, a large, high tech defence firm in St Petersburg that was broken up and privatised in early 1993, must have been repeated all over the country. According to a technician, at first the 900 workers in the television section saw privatisation as a means to increase their say in running the firm. Thus they chose to purchase 51 percent of the shares, preventing a management buy out. The shares were divided 'equally'—13 for each worker, but 56 to the director. Breaking up the firm has meant that the section's most immediate competitor is on the floor below, creating obvious contradictions such as the need for each firm to build their own identical production facility!

As a result, six months after privatisation wages were low—$25 a month, or enough to feed a typical Russian family with one child on little but bread and potatoes. To add insult to injury the dividend promised for that year failed to materialise. The workers' main complaint was that their shares had not given them any greater control, and that the old top down discipline had remained intact. 'It seems that nothing has changed,' said one. 'The director controls the management, and it's all the old faces.' Thus workers were forced to set up a new union, risking the sack to do so. The old official union had withered and died, so the initiative had to come from below.[147]

This process of seeing through the market propaganda and deciding to do something about it is a slow one, and most people still believe that there is no alternative—'the government is introducing the market the wrong way', 'the Communists are interfering'. People spend every waking hour trying to make ends meet by digging their allotment or preserving seasonally cheap fruit and vegetables, and they have little time, energy or enthusiasm for politics. They seek any escape from the everyday drudgery to which poverty condemns them. Bookstalls sell nothing but cheap detective novels and Mills and Boon, and on the TV 1970s Mexican soap operas have drawn cult followings. There is a feeling of hopelessness and paralysis. Vodka and drugs are cheap, available and universally consumed. Friends stop seeing each other because it's humiliating when there is nothing in the house to offer them. As workmates disappear to redundancy or early retirement, the remaining workers wonder if they'll be next.

The constant tension physically and mentally drives people into the ground. A single accident or illness can mean a financial catastrophe, complete ruin. People are just plain scared when they see others sink or break (Muscovites give more to beggars than Londoners). Society closes in on itself. Organised religion has not taken off—the Orthodox church is too discredited—though most people are privately religious. The success of a fanatical sect, the White Brotherhood, in bringing 60,000 teenagers from all over the former USSR to Kiev in November 1993 to witness the end of the world is an indication of the kind of despairing moods that can quickly take hold in some sections of society.

Strikes have enabled workers in some sectors to maintain a reasonable standard of living: some oil workers, for example, can earn over three times the average wage. On the other hand, a university professor earns a pittance, which is one reason for the strength of the far right in the colleges. Many families in Moscow, at least, where there are a large concentration of foreign firms, have a relative earning foreign currency and rely on them for a trickle of financial support. Their success is also taken as 'proof' that the market works in the West, so it can work for Russia. Meanwhile, between 50,000 and 100,000 people sleep rough in Moscow every night. As the crisis continues there will be increasing pressures on the ruling class to squeeze workers for more, to increase unemployment and cut wages by letting inflation rip.

Thus the situation in Russia has potential for both reaction and revolutionary change. The 'velvet revolutions' in Eastern Europe and their weaker echo in Moscow opened up for the first time in decades the possibility for workers to organise to defend themselves, a possibility denied them by the Soviet dictatorship. Rather than going too far in destroying 'socialism', the revolutions of 1989 and 1991 did not go far enough in destroying capitalism. They were stopped in their tracks as workers (understandably) put their trust in market reformers, preventing the creation of the kinds of real workers' organisation necessary to force the bosses to make concessions. This trust in the market liberals is now being destroyed. There can be no return to the past: the Soviet period is historically over, both morally and economically, and today's Russian Communist Party has cloaked itself in the flag of the Romanovs. The coming years are likely to see periods in which the Nazis can grow and their electoral wing can even enter government as in Italy, only to be thrown back by confusion in the state apparatus and by resistance from below, again as in Italy.

There is a yawning political vacuum in Russia. With the Democrats discredited and with disunity on the right, the genuine socialist tradition has the possibility of finding an audience among some sections of young people very quickly indeed. The recurrent crises at the top of society, whether it is a coup attempt, the Nazis or the war in Chechnya, constantly force people to see the direct effect of politics on their lives. With each day it gets easier to argue for socialism. The USSR had a caricature of planning and no democracy, a combination which sealed its fate. Russia now has a caricature of democracy and no planning. Workers need a combination of *real* planning with *real* democracy. As a new generation of young Russian socialists appears, eager to stop the likes of Zhirinovsky, socialists are going to find themselves with a large and attentive audience in the historical home of Bolshevism.

Notes

1 C Harman in *Socialist Review* (London), November 1993.

2 Kagarlitsky uses the 'fascist' label mainly for Russian audiences. However, in his 1992 book *The Disintegration of the Monolith* he argues that Yeltsin is ushering in a 'fascist dictatorship' led by the 'new Stalin', and refers favourably to the far-right coalition of old style Communists and Nazis—the 'Red-Browns'—as 'sincere'.

3 T Cliff's indispensable *State Capitalism in Russia* (London, 1988) was written in 1947 and has been reprinted several times and in a number of languages. Other more recent references include C Harman, *Bureaucracy and Revolution in Eastern Europe* (London, 1974); A Callinicos, 'Wage Labour and State Capitalism, *International Socialism* 12, 1981; C Harman and A Zebrowski, 'Before the Storm', *International Socialism* 39, 1988; C Harman, 'The Storm Breaks', *International Socialism* 46, 1990; D Howl, 'The Law of Value and the USSR', *International Socialism* 49, 1990; M Haynes, 'Class and Crisis: The Transition in Eastern Europe', *International Socialism* 54, 1992.

4 C Harman and M Haynes, as footnote 3 above.

5 See, for example, N Ryzhkov, *Perestroika: Istoriya Predatelstv* (Moscow, 1992) p45.

6 The extent and nature of 'planning' in the USSR have always been mythologised (for counter-examples see the second edition of Cliff's *State Capitalism* published in 1964, and M Lewin, *Political Undercurrents to Soviet Economic Debates*, London, 1975). In their more honest moments contemporary Russian economists sometimes refer to the 'bureaucratic market' or the 'administrative market' under the Soviet Union. According to Alexander Mikhalchenko, for example, formerly Soviet minister of installations and special construction works: 'When we talk about market economics we have no need to make a transition. We have always worked in market conditions, since it was always the case in our system that each unit had a large degree of autonomy, was left at its own disposal and effectively operated in a self reliant regime. This forced us to be entrepreneurs, although "entrepreneur" was a dirty word.' Unpublished interview to *VIP* magazine (Moscow, 1993).

7 *Izvestiya*, 23 July 1992. NB This article is of necessity heavily biased towards Russian sources, most of which are very politically partisan. In constructing arguments against Yeltsin and the Democrats care has been taken to use facts and figures taken from pro-market, pro-Yeltsin sources, thereby (hopefully) giving the data somewhat greater objectivity.

8 *Segodnya*, 29 November 1994.
9 J Steele, *Eternal Russia: Yeltsin, Gorbachev and the Mirage of Democracy* (London, 1994), pp302-306.
10 *Segodnya*, 30 November 1993.
11 *Segodnya*, 8 December 1993.
12 Quoted in *Socialist Review* (London), October 1993.
13 *Izvestiya*, 20 March 1993.
14 *Segodnya*, 19 November 1994.
15 Quoted in *Segodnya*, 22 January 1994.
16 *Kommersant* 15, 26 April 1994; 31, 23 August 1994.
17 See the in depth surveys in the stockbrokers' journal *Kommersant*, especially issue 31, 23 August 1994. Other figures/statements from *Izvestiya*, 17 February 1994; 9 February 1993; 29 January 1994; *Segodnya*, 1 October 1994; 4 February 1994; 27 October 1994.
18 *Finansovye Izvestiya*, 3 February 1994. The final sentence of this quote is slightly misleading: they never relinquished it in the first place.
19 *Segodnya*, 8 June 1994.
20 *Izvestiya*, 27 July 1994.
21 These figures and statements in this and the preceding paragraph are taken from, respectively: *Izvestiya*, 27 November 1992, 27 February 1993, 19 January 1993; *Segodnya*, 3 December 1993, 23 December 1993, 19 November 1994.
22 *Izvestiya*, 27 February 1993.
23 *Izvestiya*, 29 January 1993.
24 *Izvestiya*, 5 February 1993.
25 *Izvestiya*, 22 February 1993.
26 *Segodnya*, 26 January 1994.
27 *Nezavisimaya Gazeta*, 29 August 1991; Steele, op cit, p248. As Chris Harman wrote immediately after the August 1991 coup: 'Yeltsin is, in reality, seeking to placate the industrialists by putting forward the old Tsarist and Stalinist programme of Russian domination in a new guise. From being an opponent of the empire while in opposition before the coup he is rapidly moving to being its protagonist today.' *Socialist Review* (London), September 1991.
28 *Segodnya*, 9 June 1994. Turkey now enjoys rough parity with the Black Sea Fleet taken as a whole, a radical shift since the 1980s when Russia had a two to one predominance.
29 For details on Russian intervention see *Tyurma Narodov: Podyem i Upadok Sovietskoi Imperii*, and *Rossiya: Koloniya ili Kolonizator?* Socialist Solidarity Group, Moscow, 1993 and 1994 respectively.
30 *Segodnya*, 19 August 1994.
31 *Kommersant* 15, 1992. General Lebed, Yeltsin's pro-Pinochet commander in the Dnestr Republic, said that the latter 'is the key to the Balkans'. *Izvestiya*, 26 February 1993.
32 *Izvestiya*, 7 January 1992.
33 *Izvestiya*, 28 January 1992.
34 *Izvestiya*, 27 January 1993.
35 *Izvestiya*, 4 March 1993.
36 *Evropa* 4, 1994. See C Harman, 'The Storm Breaks', op cit, for details on why the USSR opened up to the world market.
37 Karaganov, op cit.
38 *Nezavisimaya Gazeta*, 24 May 1994.
39 R I Khasbulatov, *Byurokraticheskoye Gosudarstvo* (Moscow, 1991), p186.
40 *Segodnya*, 14 December 1994.
41 M Berger in the *Moscow Times*, 23 November 1994.

42 I am reliably informed by Lee Sustar of the International Socialist Organisation in New York.

43 Every year since unity west Germany has pumped $120 billion into east Germany. By comparison Russia has received only some $25 in US 'aid'.

44 *Izvestiya*, 2 March 1993.

45 One of the August 1991 coup leaders, Valentin Pavlov, for example, believes that the answer to this question is unknown (*Segodnya*, 29 November 1994). Ominously, Russia tested its new 'Topol-M' ICBM in December 1994, which will soon be added to its arsenal (*Segodnya*, 21 December 1994).

46 *Izvestiya*, 22 August 1992.

47 Ibid. Popov claims that the angry crowd outside the KGB headquarters was made up of informers who were scared that they would be revealed, and that by keeping the doors locked he (Popov) was saving the files for the people. That's as maybe. The only angry crowds I saw there during the coup were those pulling down the huge statue of Felix Dzerzhinsky opposite.

48 *Nezavisimaya Gazeta*, 17 October 1991.

49 *Segodnya*, 28 May 1994.

50 *Izvestiya*, 24 May 1994.

51 *Izvestiya*, 2 April 1993.

52 There is a peculiar argument that seems to affect exclusively Russians and left leaning Western journalists in Russia: namely that the August and October putsches were all carefully staged by Yeltsin as cunning manoeuvres to bolster his dictatorial power. But although this flies in the face of reality—Yeltsin is a *weak* figure, lurching (literally) from crisis to crisis, his grip on power and on the country slipping by the day—the argument continues to be used by people who ought to know better. A Yeltsinite conspiracy in August 1991 is the theme of *Moscow Coup* (London, 1991) by the BBC's Martin Sixmith. This position is roundly rubbished by the *Guardian's* Jonathan Steele (op cit), who then falls hopelessly for the same shabby arguments with regard to October 1993. Steele's 'strong circumstantial evidence that Yeltsin's men sprung a deadly trap' boils down, in his own admission, to the facts (i) that some policemen left their keys in their lorries while running away from an angry crowd, which encouraged the opposition to go on the offensive, and (ii) that troops defending the television centre continued firing into the dark for several hours after the armed oppositionists had dispersed (op cit, pp377-381).

There is clearly no serious case to answer here. The main point is that the conspiracy argument is used exclusively to let Rutskoi and the Red-Browns off the hook. The fact remains that the latter responded to the situation—whether planned by Yeltsin or not—with an armed attempt to seize power, assisted by Barkashov's Nazis. Lovers of conspiracy theories such as Boris Kagarlitsky must recognise that they are also dangerously close to the Nazis' accusations of 'Jewish plots'. Thus it is now common currency among the Red-Browns that Israeli troops led the assault on the White House in October 1993.

Russia is awash with conspiracy theories because the ruling class is in deep crisis and prone to bouts of acute panic. Its actions are therefore desperate and rely on state personnel who are scared, demoralised and indecisive. This is a recipe for the enormous confusion and apparent incompetence displayed by both sides during the 1991 and 1993 coups. For the record, however, let us simply restate the facts available in newspaper reports and the memoirs of leading protagonists. A fraction of the leadership around Gorbachev prepared for a coup from the end of 1990 and carried out a dress rehearsal in the Baltic States in January 1991. The August attempt was therefore no news to anybody, but was met with determined—in fact heroic—resistance on the streets and hesitancy in the bureaucracy, which sealed its downfall. Between 1991 and 1993 a power struggle took place between

Yeltsin and his former intimate collaborators, driven to desperation by the worsening economic crisis and the break-up of the empire. In October events were heading for a compromise, exactly as in April the same year when Yeltsin introduced 'special rule'—his first attempt to neutralise parliament and his latest effort to curtail parliament's authority and concentrate power in his own hands. But when a demonstration by the Red-Browns unexpectedly broke through police lines and marched triumphantly on parliament there was a wave of euphoria among the opposition, which had already armed itself and made an attempt on the General Staff building in Moscow, leaving two dead. Several hours of panic and confusion among the Yeltsinites ended when the army was finally persuaded to move against parliament.

53 See the figures in the report of the government's own Human Rights Commission, *Nezavisimaya Gazeta*, 23 July 1994.
54 *Nezavisimaya Gazeta*, 10 December 1993.
55 *Sotsialisticheskaya Initsiativa* 1, 1994.
56 *Segodnya*, 1 November 1994.
57 *Moskovsky Komsomolets*, 1 February 1994.
58 *Moskovsky Komsomolets*, 30 August 1994.
59 *Ar Rai*, 29 March 1994, quoted on Independent Television's *Itogi* programme; *Segodnya*, 26 January 1994.
60 The words are those of the deputy nationalities minister. *Segodnya*, 22 December 1994.
61 *Moskovsky Komsomolets*, 6 October 1993.
62 Quoted in *Sotsialisticheskaya Solidarnost* 2, 1994.
63 See the powerful analyses of Italian and German fascism given by Trotsky in the compilation *Fascism, Stalinism and the United Front* (London, 1989).
64 *Izvestiya*, 2 December 1994. A survey and analysis of the far right in Western Europe is provided by Chris Bambery, 'Eurofascism; the Lessons of the Past and Current Tasks', *International Socialism* 60, 1993.
65 *Izvestiya*, 19 November 1994.
66 W Lacquer, *Chernaya Sotnya: Proiskhozhdenie Russkogo Fashizma* (Moscow, 1994). (The English original is *Black Hundred: The Rise of the Extreme Right in Russia*, (New York, 1993).)
67 See *Sokol Zhirinovskogo,* Nos 1, 2, 3, 1992.
68 *Izvestiya*, 4 January 1994.
69 E Limonov, *Limonovprotiv Zhirinovskogo* (Moscow, 1994).
70 See *Izvestiya*, 4 January 1994.
71 E Limonov, op cit, p137.
72 Ibid, pp154-55. Zhirinovsky has made no attempt to denounce his former companions for their Nazi views. His response to the split comes down to calling Limonov a homosexual.
73 *Segodnya*, 22 December 1993.
74 W Sloane, 'Who's afraid of Vladimir Wolf?' *Moscow Magazine*, 1991, p47.
75 *Literaturnaya Gazeta,* 12 January 1994; *Vanity Fair,* September 1994.
76 W Lacquer, op cit, pp289-313.
77 A P Barkashov, *Azbukha Russkogo Natsionalizma* (Moscow, 1994), p66.
78 Ibid, p52.
79 *Moskovskiye Novosti*, 23 October 1994.
80 *Izvestiya*, 18 August 1994.
81 *Zavtra* 12, 1994.
82 *Izvestiya*, 11 May 1994. A detailed report in *Rabochaya Democratiya* (5, 1994) describes the hostility Barkashov is facing among workers in Cherepovetsk.
83 *Novoye Vremya* 35, 1994.
84 G A Zyuganov, *Derzhava* (Moscow, 1994), pp168-169.

85 Ibid, pp31-33, 40-44, 51, 53-54, 67, 121, 112-114.
86 Ibid, pp124-125.
87 Quoted in V Bugera, 'Sotsial-fashizm', *Marxist* 2, 1994, p30.
88 Ibid, p41.
89 E Limonov, Natsional-bolshevizm', *Zavtra* 6, 1994.
90 *Zavtra* 24, 1994.
91 Ibid. One of the groups to join Limonov was the Russian Komsomol, led by Igor Malyarov. Malyarov has succeeded in pulling a section of the Moscow anarchists into this unholy alliance, one of them a leading figure in the Initiative of Revolutionary Anarchists (IREAN).
92 D Guerin, *Fascism and Big Business* (New York, 1973), p79.
93 E Limonov, op cit, p78; *Zavtra* 6, 1994.
94 J Steele, op cit, pp341, 243.
95 See T Cliff, op cit, ch 8. W Lacquer, op cit, has a reasonable bibliography on Russian nationalism under the Soviet regime.
96 M Lewin, *Lenin's Last Struggle* (London, 1975).
97 V I Lenin, 'The Question of Nationalities or Autonomisation', in *Questions of National Policy and Proletarian Internationalism* (Moscow, 1977), p165.
98 Ibid, pp164-165.
99 M Agursky, *Ideologiya Natsional-Bolshevizma* (Paris, 1980). See also M Agursky, *National Bolshevism in the USSR* (Colorado, 1987).
100 N S Timasheff, *The Great Retreat: The Growth and Decline of Communism in Russia* (New York, 1946), p156. See also F Barghorn, *Soviet Russian Nationalism* (New York, 1956).
101 J B Dunlop, *The Faces of Contemporary Russian Nationalism* (Princeton, 1983), p12.
102 Quoted in ibid, p13.
103 N S Timasheff, op cit, pp167-73.
104 Quoted in J B Dunlop, op cit, p17.
105 D Boffa, *Istoriya Sovietskogo Soyuza* (Moscow, 1994), pp173-174. 'Big Brother', the Stalin figure in Orwell's *1984*, was actually the term publicly used by Stalin to refer to the Russian people, 'big brother' to the smaller Soviet nationalities.
106 Ibid, p332.
107 G A Zyuganov, op cit, p73-74.
108 C Harman and A Zebrowski, op cit; C Harman, 'The Storm Breaks', op cit. A contemporary Russian source confirming Harman and Zebrowski's analysis and giving a mass of additional detail is A Avtorkhanov, *Imperiya Kremlya: Sovietsky Tip Kolonialisma* (Vilnius, 1990).
109 A Yanov, *Russkaya Ideya i 2000 God* (Paris, 1980). The English edition is *The Russian Challenge and the Year 2000* (Oxford, 1986). J B Dunlop, op cit.
110 J B Dunlop, op cit, pp46-47.
111 W Lacquer, op cit, p110.
112 Glazunov's 1994 exhibition in Moscow was opened by Boris Yeltsin and advertised all over the city. It attracted tens of thousands of visitors.
113. A Yanov, op cit, pp163-167.
114 Ibid, p115.
115. See Yanov and Dunlop, op cit.
116 Quoted in M Agursky, pp225-226.
117 L D Trotsky, 'Termidor i antisemitizm', in *Prestupleniya Stalina* (Moscow, 1994), pp219-220.
118 M Agursky, op cit, pp258-259.
119 R S Wistrich, *Antisemitism: The Longest Hatred* (London, 1992), pp175-176.

120 Centre for Political and Economic History of Russia, *Nesostoyavshiisya Yubilei: Pochemu SSSR ne Otprazdnoval svoego 70-letiya?* (Moscow, 1992), pp312-313; R S Wistrich, op cit, p178.
121 W Lacquer, op cit, pp165-166.
122 Ibid, p165.
123 J Steele (op cit), title of chapter 13.
124 D Stephan, *Russkiye Fashisty: Tragediya i Fars v Emigratsii* (Moscow, 1992), p402. In quoting Rodzaevsky I do not want to suggest that Stalinism was a brand of fascism—its social base and road to power were very different from those of Hitler or Mussolini—but simply to show that points of contact with Stalinism exist for today's Russian Nazis, enabling them to incorporate the Soviet period into their nationalist ideology. Stalinism in Russia and Eastern Europe—but emphatically not in those countries where it did not take power—was the ideology of the counter-revolutionary bureaucracy of an isolated workers' state.
125 For a time Kagarlitsky even issued a bulletin called *Moscovsky Leiborist* (*Moscow Labourist*), which must have puzzled some of its readers, since there is nothing sounding even remotely similar to the English word 'labour' in the Russian language.
126 Conference document quoted in *Socialist Review* (London), February 1992.
127 *Solidarnost* 17, 1992.
128 *Moskovskiye Novosti*, 24 July 1994.
129 *Segodnya*, 22 September 1994.
130 *Nezavisimaya Gazeta*, 28 July 1994.
131 *Moskovskiye Novosti*, 30 October 1994.
132 Ibid.
133 *Socialist Review* (London), February 1992.
134 *Solidarnost* 13, 1992.
135 Ibid.
136. C Harman, 'The Storm Breaks', op cit, pp75-77.
137 See also W Lacquer, op cit, pp360-363.
138 T Cliff, 'Balance of Powerlessness', *Socialist Review* (London), September 1991, pp10-11.
139 C Harman, 'The Storm Breaks', op cit.
130 *Izvestiya*, 20 July 1994.
141. G Vachnadze, *Voennye Mafii Kremlya* (Moscow, 1994), p230.
142 In later interviews Rutskoi called Barkashov a promising young politician and remarked in response to a journalist's observation that Barkashov wears a swastika: 'You don't know the ancient runes. That's not a swastika!' *Novoye Vremya*, op cit.
143 *Segodnya*, 13 October 1994.
144 G Vachnadze, op cit, p224. 'Concerning the potential for a mass Nazi movement in Russia, it might be objected that there is no "middle class" as such in Russia, at least not in the classical sense of the term, and therefore a limited social base for the Nazis. However, Hitler's Nazis conquered in a country in which state capitalism was at its most advanced. Trotsky was clear in identifying that: 'The main army of fascism still consists of the petty bourgeoisie and the *new middle class:* the small artisans and shopkeepers of the cities, the petty officials, the employers, the technical personnel, the intelligentsia...' (*Fascism, Stalinism and the United Front,* op cit, pp69-70, emphasis added). Though Russia has until recently been short on private shop-keepers, small businessmen and so on, the *new middle class* consisting of the state and former Party bureaucracy is immense. Trotsky characterised fascism as the mass movement of the 'crazed petty-bourgeoisie'; fascism in Russia is the movement of the crazed petty bureaucrat, the new middle class gone mad.'

145 See W Lacquer, op cit, pp289-313.
146 *Izvestiya* 18 October 1994.
147 D Crouch, 'Breaking Up or Uniting?' *St Petersburg News* 3, 1993, pp20-22.

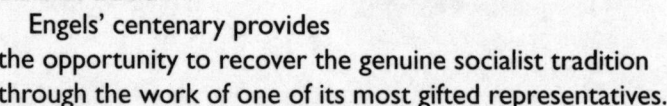

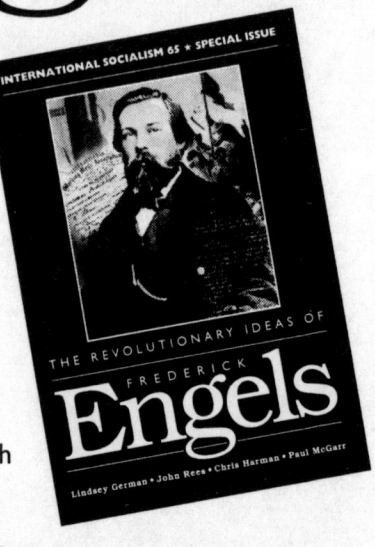

Cruel and unusual punishment: the politics of crime in the United States

PHIL GASPER

Both houses of the United States Congress passed President Clinton's $30 billion Omnibus Crime Bill in August 1994 by wide margins. A few days later the president signed 'the largest, most expensive crime bill in history' into law.[1] Clinton had in fact worked overtime to ensure the legislation's passage. The core of his proposal included a sizeable increase in the number of police and an extension of police powers, a further expansion of prison building, and a series of provisions mandating harsher punishments for those found guilty in federal courts. In order to win over Republican votes,[2] Clinton reduced the modest amount of preventative social spending originally contained in the bill. He also jettisoned a provision supported by the Congressional Black Caucus which would have permitted statistical evidence of racial bias to be used by defendants appealing against death penalty sentences. The final legislation was a major victory for all those who argue that crime in the streets is not a consequence of poverty, inequality, bad housing, disintegrating schools, high unemployment and other social causes, but is instead largely the result of anti-social individuals, who must be punished severely in order to deter others and protect the public.[3]

By any reasonable standards, Clinton's crime bill (which eventually ran to 412 pages) is draconian. Among its provisions are the following:[4] $10.8 billion in federal matching funds for local governments to hire 100,000 new police officers over the next five years, $10 billion for the construction of new federal prisons, an expansion of the number of federal crimes to which the death penalty applies from two to 58 (the bill also eliminated an existing statute which prohibited the execution of mentally incapacitated defendants), a so called 'three strikes' proposal which mandates life sentences for anyone convicted of three 'violent' felonies (or even 'attempts' to commit such felonies) or of two 'violent' offences and one 'serious' drug felony, a section which allows children as young as 13 to be tried as adults, and the creation of special courts able to deport non-citizens alleged to be 'engaged in terrorist activity' on the basis of secret evidence.

But while the federal crime bill is severe, it is by no means a policy aberration in US terms. In fact, the legislation represents simply the latest stage in a 'law and order' backlash which has been moving at full speed since the early 1980s and which has historical roots going back over 30 years.

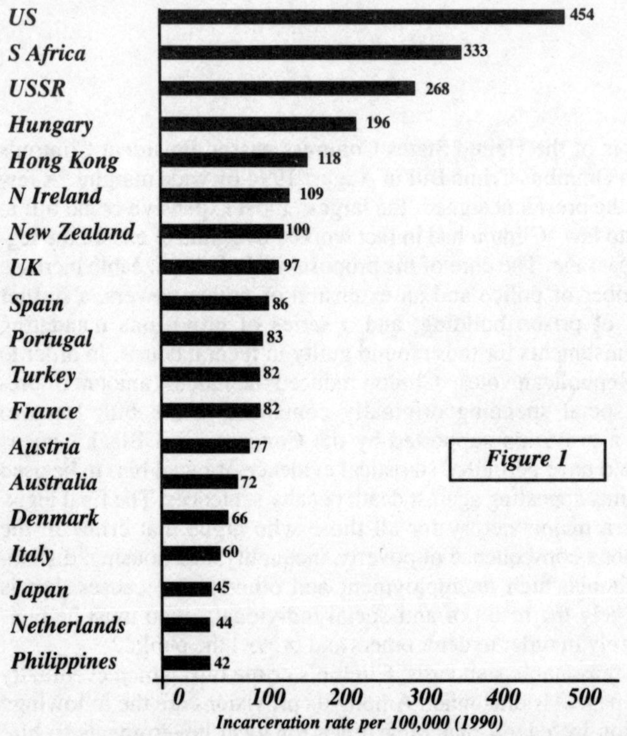

Figure 1

(Sources: S Whitman 'The Crime of Black Imprisonment', Z Magazine, May 1992; W Chambliss, 'Policing the Ghetto Undeclass', Social problems, May 1994).

Crime hysteria

Over the past decade and a half the United States has experienced a massive increase in the size of what one criminologist has dubbed the 'crime control industry'.[5] Between 1980 and 1990 the number of police in the country doubled, and in a single year (1990) the Federal Bureau of Investigation increased in size by 25 percent.[6] The increase in the level of incarceration has been even more dramatic. Since 1980 the total prison population at federal, state and local levels has tripled to over 1 million,[7] more people than live in San Francisco or Washington DC. The female prison population doubled between 1985 and 1992.[8] The incarceration rate in the US, exceptionally high at the beginning of this period, is today almost off the scale compared with any other advanced capitalist country (see Figure 1). The situation has become so extreme that 40 states were under federal court order in 1992 to reduce overcrowding in their prisons.[9] The worst case is California, where the prison population grew by 460 percent between 1977 and 1992, from less than 20,000 to more than 110,000. The California prison system is now not only by far the largest in the country, it is, if we exclude the US as a whole, the second biggest in the world after China.[10]

The numbers involved in other sectors of the criminal justice system are even more enormous. In the middle of 1991 almost 2 percent of the US population (over 4.4 million people) were in prison, on probation, on parole, or under some other form of control—one and a half times more than the population of Chicago. In 1989 more than 14 million people in the US were arrested.[11] State and local governments today spend more on the criminal justice system than on the education budget. The criminologist William Chambliss reports that:

> *Nationwide, expenditures on criminal justice increased by 150 percent between 1972 and 1986, while expenditures on education increased by 46 percent. Between 1969 and 1989 per capita spending on criminal justice in US cities...rose from $34 to $120 and county expenditures as a percentage of total budget rose from 10 to 15 percent between 1973 and 1989. State expenditures showed even greater increases, rising tenfold from per capita expenditures on police and corrections of $8 in 1969 to $80 in 1989. State government expenditure for building prisons increased 593 percent in actual dollars. Spending on corrections—prison building, maintenance, and parole—has more than doubled in the last ten years.*[12]

This massive growth in the crime industry, however, may only be the beginning. A series of recent laws passed at both federal and state levels (including, of course, the Clinton crime bill discussed above) will increase both the number of police and the prison population even further.

Washington state passed a 'three strikes' law in November 1993 which mandates life imprisonment for anyone found guilty of a third felony offence. A similar law was passed in California a few months later, and about 30 other states are also considering some form of it.[13] Numerous states—including California, Florida, Illinois and Minnesota—have also enacted laws which make it easier to charge juvenile offenders (in some cases as young as ten years old) in the same way as they can adults.[14] In California it is estimated that by the end of the century the prison population will nearly double again and that the state will need to build 20 new prisons over the next five years. By the year 2027 the prison population in the state will reach 275,000 according to the California Department of Corrections.[15]

Crime hysteria in the US has not impacted on all sections of the population equally. As Chambliss notes:

> *It is minorities, especially young African Americans and Latinos, who are disproportionately arrested, convicted and sentenced to prison. In 1991, African-American males between the ages of 15 and 34 made up 14 percent of the population and more than 40 percent of the people in prison... In Washington DC and Baltimore, 40 to 50 percent of all black males between the ages of 18 and 35 are either in prison, jail, on probation or parole, or there is a warrant for their arrest.*[16]

These figures are quite astonishing. The rate of imprisonment for black men in the US is 7.4 times higher than for white people and actually over four times that of black men in South Africa before the dismantling of apartheid (see Figure 2). There are now more young black men (aged 20 to 29) under the control of the criminal justice system than in college, and one out of every four black men will be imprisoned at some point in his life (not counting stays in local jails).[17] Blacks are also three times more likely than whites to be killed by the police.[18]

The roots of US crime policy

How are we to explain the vast growth of the US crime industry in recent years? One possible explanation is that the increase is due to a rising level of crime. But while the crime rate, particularly the level of violent crime, is certainly higher in the US than in other advanced industrialised countries,[19] it is simply a myth that crime is on the increase in the US. According to Chambliss, 'The best available data, the findings of victim surveys conducted every year since 1973, show that the crime rate has not changed significantly in the last 20 years',[20] with violent crimes and murder being no exception to this general trend. Indeed, if anything,

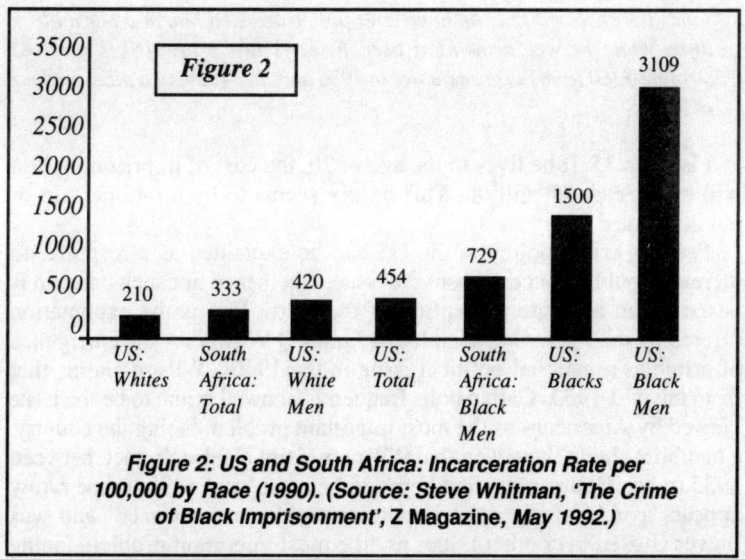

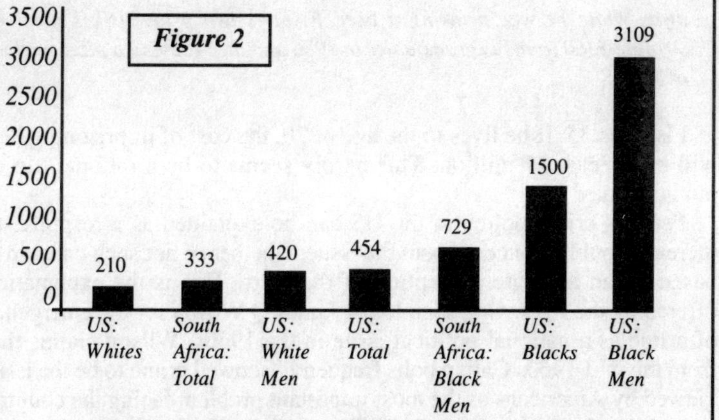

Figure 2: US and South Africa: Incarceration Rate per 100,000 by Race (1990). (Source: Steve Whitman, 'The Crime of Black Imprisonment', Z Magazine, May 1992.)

crime rates have decreased slightly since the early 1980s, particularly in the predominantly white suburbs, where a 'resident was 13 percent more likely to be a victim of violent crime in 1973' than today, and where 'crimes like theft and burglary have declined substantially'.[21]

Moreover, even if the crime rate were rising, increasing the size of police forces and lengthening prison sentences hardly seem to make sense in rational policy terms. Research shows that the police are ineffective in preventing crime,[22] and according to the American Bar Association's Task Force on Crime, 'There is no solid evidence to support the conclusion that sending more convicted offenders to prison for longer periods of time deters others from committing crime.'[23] Meanwhile, the 'three strike' frenzy threatens to bust state budgets while tens of thousands are locked up for relatively minor offences. In the states which have passed such laws this has already begun. In California, Duane Silva, a retarded 23 year old, has been sent to prison for the rest of his life for stealing a video recorder from a friend's house.[24] Others have been charged with third strike offences that include stealing 50 cents and sitting in a stolen truck.[25] According to a report by the Center on Juvenile and Criminal Justice, 75 percent of third strike cases in Los Angeles County involve a third offence that is non-violent and non-serious.[26]

In Washington state, Larry Fisher was sent to prison for life for:

...putting his finger in his pocket, pretending it was a gun, and robbing a sandwich shop of $151. An hour later police arrested him at a bar a block away while he was drinking a beer. Fisher's two prior strikes involved stealing $360 from his grandfather in 1986 and then robbing a pizza parlour of $100.[27]

Fisher is 35. If he lives to the age of 70, the cost of imprisoning him will be at least $1 million. This hardly seems to be a rational use of public money.

Perhaps crime policy in the US can be explained as a response to increased public concern about the issue, whether or not such concern is based on an accurate perception of the facts. This is the explanation offered by the right wing sociologist James Q Wilson for the emergence of crime as a national political issue in the 1960s. Wilson claims that from the mid-1960s Gallup polls frequently showed crime to be the issue viewed by Americans as the most important problem facing the country. Chambliss shows, however, that Wilson's claim is false. In fact, between 1935 (when Gallup polls first began to be taken) and 1993 'crime rarely appears as one of the most important problems mentioned' and was 'never chosen over other issues as "the most important problem facing the country".'[28]

More recently there has been a shift. In early 1994 a *New York Times* front page story announced that 'Crime Is Becoming Nation's Top Fear',[29] and the University of Chicago's General Social Survey conducted in the spring of the same year reported that fighting crime came highest in a list of the public's spending priorities.[30] But recent increased concern over crime is quite obviously an effect, and not the cause, of the massive attention given to the issue by politicians of both main political parties and by the corporate media. According to one report:

Crime took up more than two and a half hours (157 minutes) a month on the three nightly network news shows from October 1993 until January 1994. In the three years ending with January 1992, by contrast, these network shows spent 67 minutes a month on crime stories. And the coverage has taken on a shrill tabloid tone, designed to evoke fear, as with NBC Nightly News' regular feature 'Society Under Siege'.[31]

The saturation coverage clearly has an impact, since a recent poll found that 65 percent of the population get their information on crime from the media.[32]

Chambliss suggests that there are two underlying reasons for the growing crime hysteria in the US. First, there is the lobbying power of law enforcement agencies and other sectors of the 'crime industry'. 'On those rare occasions when a mayor or governor suggests cutting justice expenditures or even holding steady the number of police officers, propaganda, politicking and arm twisting by police officer associations...and lobbyists with vested interests in supplying equipment and prison facilities quickly reverse the decision'.[33] No doubt such activities sometimes play a role, but on their own they cannot be the only or even the main explanation. Teachers' unions, building contractors, school textbook publishers and other groups with a vested interest in increased education expenditure presumably have comparable influence to the crime lobby, yet they have not been able to prevent sharp cuts in education spending in recent years.

Far more important is a second factor mentioned by Chambliss: the way in which an emphasis on 'crime control' has come to serve ruling class interests in the US, both ideologically and by giving the state increased powers of repression to deal with the most economically deprived section of the population and other potential troublemakers.[34] As he puts it:

> *The politicisation of crime by conservative politicians occurred at a time when the country was deeply divided over the Vietnam War and civil rights. In this historical context crime became a smokescreen behind which other issues could be relegated less important. Crime served as well as legitimation for legislation designed primarily to suppress political dissent.*[35]

This is exactly right. However, there are some important differences between the 1960s on the one hand, and the 1980s and the 1990s on the other. In the earlier period the main use of the crime issue was ideological. In particular, crime was used as a weapon to limit and attempt to roll back the gains of the Civil Rights movement, as well as to attack the other social movements of the 1960s. More recently, however, as economic inequalities in the US have deepened, the main purpose of crime policy has become less subtle. Significant sections of the population—notably black and Latino youths in urban centres—have been criminalised, as inner cities across the country have been turned into virtual police states. As social spending in the US falls dramatically with more cuts to come and well paid full time jobs become more scarce[36], crime control has become an increasingly important part of social policy. The ideological function, however, has not disappeared. Crime policy continues to play an important role in perpetuating racism, reinforcing the central division in the US working class and thus making a unified fightback against the root causes of unemployment, poverty and inequality more difficult.[37]

High rates of imprisonment for minority youth can be explained in part by the fact that they are disproportionately represented in the most economically deprived sections of society, but also reflect the way in which the legal system discriminates against suspccts on the basis of their colour.

The 'law and order' backlash in the 1960s

Before the 1960s crime was seldom an issue in national and, in particular, presidential politics in the United States.[38] Crime prevention, detection and punishment, were generally seen as matters for state, county and local governments. It was not until the presidential election of 1964 that crime became a major national issue. The far right Republican candidate, Barry Goldwater, who was a fanatical anti-Communist in foreign policy, and who opposed civil rights legislation at home, made 'law and order' a central part of his campaign. In his acceptance speech at the Republican convention, Goldwater warned of 'violence in the streets' and of the 'growing menace to personal safety, to life, to limb and to property'.[39] All of this was little more than a thinly veiled attack on the Civil Rights movement which was fighting against segregation in the South and racial discrimination in the North. In a speech later in the campaign he was more explicit:

> *Our wives, all women, feel unsafe on our streets. And in encouragement of even more abuse of the law, we have the appalling spectacle of this country's ambassador to the United Nations* [Adlai Stevenson] *actually telling an audience...that 'in the great struggle to advance human civil rights, even a jail sentence is no longer a dishonour but a proud achievement.' Perhaps we are destined to see in this law-loving land people running for office not on their stainless records but on their prison record.*[40]

But Goldwater's rhetoric proved to be too extreme for the majority of the American voters,[41] and he lost the election to Lyndon Johnson in a landslide. Significantly, however, five of the six states which Goldwater carried were in the South, which had been solidly Democratic for the 100 years before.

Johnson himself was impressed by Goldwater's use of the law and order card, and adopted some of the rhetoric himself as part of a so called 'war on crime'. But it was politicians further to the right who made most of the running with the issue. As the 1960s progressed, 'law and order' became the rallying cry of right wingers opposed to the Civil Rights, anti-war and student movements, as well as a convenient way to make coded appeals to racists, particularly in the South. The master of this form of politics was George Wallace, the arch-segregationist Democrat governor of Alabama, who ran for president as an independent in 1968 and won 13 percent of the vote. Wallace's racism was barely hidden. In 1967, for example, he told an audience in South Carolina that 'Supreme Court decisions have made it almost impossible for police to arrest a criminal. Politicians are always trying to explain why some people don't obey the law—because they didn't have any watermelon when they were small children'.[42] On another occasion he openly blamed crime on blacks: 'Crime is one of the reasons race relations have deteriorated'.[43] Above all, Wallace linked concern over street crime to attacks on the Civil Rights movement and the black ghetto rebellions of the mid-1960s. As he put it in one speech, 'The lawlessness emanating from lawless edicts [ie civil rights legislation] now stalk [sic] in our streets, riot in our cities, intimidate our Congress and threaten the very order of our civilisation'.[44]

Wallace had no real chance of winning the presidency in 1968, but his successful manipulation of the law and order issue was taken up enthusiastically by the election's eventual winner, the Republican Richard M Nixon. As Wallace correctly noted, 'Law and order is an issue in the 1968 presidential campaign and I was the first candidate to speak out on it a year and a half ago'.[45] Nixon, unlike Wallace, was no homegrown Southern racist, but a Northern politician who had gone on record in opposition to segregation. But Nixon also had a record as a political opportunist willing to use any tactics necessary to win an election, and he was quite happy to borrow Wallace's law and order rhetoric if that would help win votes in the South.[46] This was part of Nixon's 'Southern strategy', later spelled out in detail in Kevin Phillips's 1969 book, *The Emerging Republican Majority*.[47] The idea was to learn the lessons of the Goldwater campaign, and to consolidate a solid bloc of Republican voters by winning over Southerners attracted to Wallace, social conservatives, and white ethnics. As part of this strategy Nixon 'made law and order his central theme, and played it hard to enthusiastic audiences who greeted his punch line with vigorous applause: "Some of our courts have gone too far in weakening the peace forces as against the criminal forces".'[48]

Nixon's running mate, Spiro T Agnew, the governor of Maryland, followed Wallace in linking fear of street crime to attacks on the black liberation and anti-war movements. 'When I talk about troublemakers', he said in a September speech, 'I'm talking about muggers and criminals in the streets, assassins of political leaders, draft evaders and flag burners, campus militants, hecklers and demonstrators against candidates for public office and looters and burners of cities.'[49] Nixon himself wrote in an article published in *Readers' Digest* that America was 'the most lawless and violent [nation] in the history of free peoples', blaming this on the 'growing tolerance of lawlessness' by civil rights organisations and 'the increasing public acceptance of civil disobedience'.[50]

Early on in the campaign Nixon attacked the President's National Advisory Commission on Civil Disorders (the Kerner Commission), set up by President Johnson after the Detroit riot in 1967, for blaming urban disturbances on poverty and white racism. 'One of the major weaknesses of the president's commission', Nixon told a radio interviewer in New Hampshire, 'is that it, in effect, blames everybody for the riots except the perpetrators of the riots.' Nixon's own solution would be 'to meet force with force', and he demanded 'retaliation against the perpetrators of violence' that was 'swift and sure'. According to Ambrose:

> *Nixon was pleased with his effort, and even more so with the response. He wrote* [to former president] *Eisenhower, delightedly, that 'I have found great audience response to this theme* [law and order] *in all parts of the country, including areas like New Hampshire where there is virtually no race problem and relatively little crime'.*[51]

During the campaign, Nixon's Democratic opponent, vice-president Hubert Humphrey, replied that 'for every jail Mr Nixon wants to build I'd like to build a house for a family. And for every policeman he wants to hire I'd like to hire another good teacher'.[52] Nixon responded by accusing Humphrey of having 'a personal attitude of indulgence and permissiveness toward the lawless', and arguing that by identifying poverty as the root cause of crime, the vice-president was showing sympathy for criminals.[53]

Nixon won the 1968 election narrowly and was then faced with the task of converting his law and order rhetoric into concrete proposals. As the historian Michael Genovese notes, however, 'Nixon never developed a thought-out, coherent anti-crime programme' and 'the politics of crime took precedence over the policy'.[54] Bob Haldeman, Nixon's chief of staff, recorded a March 1970 meeting in which the president told him, in a memo, 'Problem is not what we do—but the appearance/not getting the points we should on crime'.[55] In a June 1971 meeting Nixon told Haldeman, 'Look in terms of how create issues/need an enemy, controversy/drugs and law enforcement. May be one/esp since so weak in polls'.[56] Shortly afterwards the administration intensified the war on drugs, but an internal memo by one aide later conceded that 'nothing really was accomplished'. Nevertheless, as Genovese points out, the policy 'did generate a great deal of favourable publicity for the administration. The pattern of devising policies for their favourable press as a way to boost the image of Nixon as tough on crime replaced substantive policy as a means of reducing crime'.[57] It also served as a way of distracting attention from other issues such as the rapidly deteriorating economy and the continuing war in Vietnam.[58]

The Reagan-Bush years and the war on drugs

Nixon used the crime issue for primarily ideological ends, but the exposure and cover up of the Watergate break in and Nixon's eventual resignation in 1974 turned public attention towards crime and corruption in high places and away from crime in the streets. But the law and order rhetoric of Goldwater, Wallace and Nixon made a comeback, and indeed reached new heights, with the election of Ronald Reagan to the presidency in 1980. Reagan had already won a reputation for being 'tough on crime', as well as an opponent of civil rights and of the various social movements, during his period as governor of California from 1966 to 1974. Like Goldwater, Reagan opposed the federal Civil Rights Act of 1964 and the Voting Rights Act of 1965. His 1966 campaign to be governor began in the wake of the 1965 Watts riots in Los Angeles and from the start played on racial tensions. As one Reagan aide put it at the time, 'We'll settle for the white vote.' Reagan opposed legislating an end to racial discrimination in housing on the grounds that this would compromise the property rights of owners. In a speech to the California Real Estate Association he claimed that black allegations of discrimination were simply 'staged attempts to rent homes, when in truth there was no real intention of renting, only of causing trouble.'

Reagan became a master of linking the law and order theme with covert, and sometimes not so covert, racial messages. He described the black ghetto rebellions of the 1960s as 'riots of the law breakers and the mad dogs against the people'. Commenting on the assassination of civil rights leader Martin Luther King Jr in 1968, Reagan blamed King's own advocacy of civil disobedience: this 'great tragedy began when we began compromising with law and order and people started choosing which laws they'd break.' One Reagan radio commercial of this period warned:

> *Every day the jungle draws a little closer. Our city streets are jungle paths after dark... Man's determination to live under the protection of the law has pushed back the jungle down through the centuries. But the jungle is always there, and somehow it seems much closer than we have known it in the years preceding. With all our science and sophistication...the jungle still is waiting to take over. The man with the badge holds it back.*[59]

After he became president, Reagan worked diligently to give the 'man with the badge' increased powers. During his first term in office his Justice Department lobbied the Supreme Court to strengthen the power of government and weaken individual rights. According to one commentator, 'Whatever the administration asked' from the court, 'it almost always received'.[60] During the court's 1983-1984 term, for example, it ruled that preventive detention for people not yet charged, let alone convicted, of a crime is constitutional, restricted prisoners' rights and allowed evidence seized illegally to be used in criminal trials. 'I was quite struck by the fact that the Statue of Liberty was in shackles and being dismantled', commented Harvard Law School Professor Laurence H Tribe. 'In one sphere after another, the court has affirmed the almost boundless authority of government over the individual and of the executive over the other branches'.[61]

It was also under Reagan that the myth of the 'career criminal' who cannot be rehabilitated and who must be locked up permanently, took firm hold. In fact, as one commentator notes, there are few professional criminals:

> *Most of the people in prison are not evil or professional criminals. They tend to be poor people with emotional, drug, or alcohol problems who are caught doing something stupid. The 'professional career criminal' tends to be a media myth, unless we count savings and loan bankers, Fortune 500 companies, Oliver North and Company, etc.*[62]

For an administration eager to give the courts and the prison system an increased role in social policy, however, the myth was a useful one. Legislation such as the federal Armed Career Criminal Act of 1988, which mandated 25 years without parole for a third time felon found in possession of a firearm, helped boost the federal prison population from 24,363 in 1980 to 60,751 a decade later,[63] despite no increase in the rate of crime.

The central vehicle for crime policy under both Reagan and his successor George Bush was a newly invigorated 'war on drugs', directed in particular at minority communities in the inner cities. There is in fact a long history of using drug laws in the US to criminalise and harass members of non-white racial groups, the Chinese in the 19th century, Mexicans and blacks in the 20th. Despite rhetoric to the contrary, the same was true of the Reagan-Bush crusade. As a report in one mainstream newspaper put it in 1990, 'The nation's war on drugs has, in effect, become a war on black people'.[64]

Although a lower percentage of blacks and Latinos use drugs than do whites, and 80 percent of cocaine consumers (and most of the distributors) are white, enforcement efforts were concentrated (and indeed continue to be focused) on addicts and small time traffickers in the inner cities. Moreover, under federal law someone convicted of selling 5 grams or more of crack cocaine—the form of the drug most widely used by the poor—worth around $125 receives a mandatory sentence of at least five years. By comparison, one would have to be convicted of possessing 500 grams of powdered cocaine—the form of the drug generally used by middle class whites—worth nearly $50,000, to be given the same sentence.[65] The blatant racism could hardly be clearer.

The war on drugs was mainly responsible for the huge increase in the US prison population in the 1980s. By 1992 more people were in federal prison for drug crimes than for all crimes at the time Reagan took office.[66] Yet none of this had anything to do with either reducing crime or ending drug addiction. Much crime is in fact generated by criminalising narcotics, since this creates a profitable black market and the possibility of deadly turf wars. Meanwhile, as funds pour into law enforcement, budgets for rehabilitation programmes are slashed.

The collapse of liberalism

While it was Reagan and Bush who pushed the war on drugs, and the right wing agenda on crime more generally, they were helped enormously by the collapse of any kind of liberal opposition to their policies. Indeed, as Mike Davis observes, after George Bush trounced Michael Dukakis in the 1988 presidential election largely by accusing him of being soft on crime, 'a whole generation of Democrats [now believe] that their political survival depends on being even more bloodthirsty than Republicans'.[67]

In the 1992 presidential election Clinton attempted to outflank Bush from the right on crime. He posed for photos with the police at every opportunity, called for more officers to be hired, and advocated 'boot camps' for young offenders.[68] Other leading Democrats followed his lead. By the time Clinton's crime bill was passed last year, George Mitchell, the Democratic Senate Majority Leader at the time, was declaring, 'On crime, the time is over when in fact or perception the Republican Party is seen as the party tough on crime. It's the Democrats.'[69]

Even Democrats with a more liberal reputation than Clinton or Mitchell have jumped on the bandwagon. The black Democratic leadership in Congress backed Clinton's crime bill,[70] and, as one commentator noted a few years ago, 'it's sometimes hard to tell the difference between the anti-drug rhetoric of, say, Jesse Jackson and George Bush'.[71] During the 1993 mayoral election in Los Angeles, the 'liberal' former council member Michael Woo, an Asian-American, essentially ran on the same platform as his right wing opponent, Richard Riordan. Both agreed, for instance, that the city's top priority was 3,000 new cops. Mike Davis observes:

> *Woo imitated rather than challenged Riordan by hammering away on identical law and order themes. Against a background of rising white hysteria about a new riot in the wake of the Rodney King or Reginald Denny beating*

trials, the councilperson merely seemed to ratify paranoid perceptions of the inner city. It was a strategy that one of his campaign workers defended as 'snake charming'.[72]

On the day of the election, however, Woo's strategy proved to be a failure. Black and Latino voters stayed home in record numbers, while the majority of whites preferred to vote for a genuine right winger rather than his post-liberal carbon copy. Riordan won by a clear margin.

The retreat of the liberals, however, is not merely the result of cowardice or stupidity. Liberals are committed to reforming the existing system, not overthrowing it. In periods of sustained economic growth it is possible for them to fund education, housing, health and other programmes that address the social conditions which breed crime. In periods of economic crisis, however, this is no longer possible. The options then become either a radical break with the priorities of a society geared to generating profits for the few, or a shift to the right. Establishment liberals invariably choose the latter course. The options are especially stark in the present economic conjuncture. As the economist Michael Yates observes:

[US society is] *coming apart at the seams. The national unemployment rate has not been below 5 percent since 1973, which means that at no time during the Reagan 'boom' of the 1980s were there fewer than 6 million unemployed by the government's own count. The purchasing power of our weekly earnings is no higher now than it was in 1967. We have been able to maintain our standards of living only by working more hours or sending more family members into the workforce. Yet in the last few years family income has also begun to fall. Our children have not faced a bleaker future since the Great Depression of the 1930s... Average real family income fell for the poorest 60 percent of all families between 1977 and 1990, but it increased by 33.2 percent for the richest 20 percent and by a staggering 95.1 percent for the richest 1 percent. The government poverty level is barely enough to live on, yet there are more than 30 million people living below it. It is estimated that by the year 2000 one of every three children will be poor.*[73]

The pressures of international competition are rapidly turning the United States into a two tier society in which large sections of the population face a future of low paying jobs, unemployment and little hope. In the absence of decent jobs or social programmes some other way is needed to keep them in line. Politicians of both major political parties have turned to crime control as a solution to this problem.

The death penalty

No article on criminal justice in the United States would be complete without some discussion of the use of the death penalty. The US is the only advanced industrialised country which still regularly employs capital punishment. In most of Western Europe there have been no executions for over 25 years, and the death penalty remains on the books only for exceptional crimes, such as treason during time of war. Even South Africa has had a moratorium on executions over the past few years.

For a time it appeared as if the US would follow the example of Western European countries and abolish the death penalty. In 1972, after a long campaign led by civil rights groups which highlighted the extreme racial bias in the application of capital punishment, the Supreme Court ruled in a case known as Furman v Georgia that existing death penalty statutes were unconstitutional because they could be applied in essentially arbitrary ways. In 1976, however, the court reinstated capital punishment when it ruled that new and more elaborate death penalty laws passed by several states in the early 1970s were constitutional.[74] The court's effective reversal of its earlier decision was symbolic of a general shift to the right in US politics as the movements of the 1960s and early 1970s ebbed and the post-war boom came to an end. Since 1977 there have been close to 200 executions in the US. Over 2,500 people are awaiting their fate on death row today.

Yet the arguments against capital punishment remain compelling. As one commentator observes, 'There is no data supporting the notion that the death penalty deters capital crimes and much evidence showing that it is applied in racist and class-biased ways, almost exclusively against racial minorities and poor whites'.[75] It was the arbitrariness of capital punishment—the fact that the death penalty was often applied in one case while not in another identical case—that led to the 1972 ruling against it. Current statutes are supposed to be applied impartially, but there is overwhelming evidence that they are not. African-Americans make up about 12 percent of the US population, yet 40 percent of prisoners on death row are black and 50 percent are non-white.[76] The Death Penalty Information Centre reports that, although 'blacks are homicide victims at a rate six times greater than whites, 95 percent of those executed in 1990 murdered white people'.[77] Between 1977 and 1992 more than 40 blacks were executed for killing whites, while only one white who killed a black was treated the same way.[78] In a 1987 decision, however, the rapidly rightward moving Supreme Court ruled that statistical evidence of this kind is irrelevant. In order for a death sentence to be overturned, racial (or other) bias must be proved in that particular case—a virtually impossible task.[79]

According to one poll, 58 percent of Americans are disturbed by the fact that innocent people may be executed,[80] but there can be no doubt that numerous innocent people have been put to death. Since 1900 at least 416 demonstrably innocent people have been convicted of capital crimes in the US. These, of course, are only the cases we know about. Since 1973 alone at least 43 people on death row have subsequently been found innocent on appeal.[81]

But these are the lucky ones. Once a defendant has been found guilty, it is extraordinarily difficult for him or her to have the conviction overturned. Before the initial trial defendants are (in theory at least) assumed to be innocent, and the prosecution must demonstrate guilt beyond a reasonable doubt. After conviction, however, the presumption of guilt shifts, and the defendant must produce 'clear and compelling' evidence to be found innocent. Moreover, in the majority of states there is a time limit for the introduction of new evidence. In 17 states new evidence must be submitted within 60 days of the initial conviction, otherwise it is ineligible. As Michael Ross notes, these rules are inflexible:

> *Roger Coleman's volunteer attorneys uncovered evidence of his innocence after his conviction for murder. However, his appeal based on this newly discovered evidence was filed three days late, and because of this error,* ***made by his attorneys****, the Virginia state courts and federal appeals courts refused to hear the new evidence. Roger Coleman was executed on May 22, 1992.*[82]

Recent Supreme Court decisions have made the situation even worse, denying appeals on narrow technical grounds in the face of new evidence of innocence. In 1993 the court denied the appeal of Leonel Torres Herrera who was convicted in 1982 in Texas of the murder of two police officers. Some years later it came to light that Herrera's brother Raul, who had subsequently died, had confessed to the murders, and Raul's son testified that he had seen his father commit the killings. This evidence was not even considered, because the cut off date for new evidence had long since passed. The Supreme Court upheld this decision, ruling that Herrera's claim of 'actual innocence' was not relevant to the question of whether or not he had received a fair trial. In a dissenting opinion, Justice Harry Blackmun—previously a proponent of capital punishment—attacked the ruling, arguing that the 'execution of a person who can show that he is innocent comes perilously close to simple murder.' Herrera was executed on 12 May 1993.

Earlier this year the court made an even more egregious ruling on another Texas case. In 1987 Jesse Dewayne Jacobs was sentenced to death for murder on the basis of a confession which he subsequently retracted. After this retraction the state prosecutor conceded that Jacobs was innocent and that the murder was in fact committed by his sister, who was then tried and convicted for the crime. Despite the second conviction, however, Jacobs' death penalty still stood. An appeals court acknowledged that the verdicts of the two trials were at odds, but declared that 'it is not for us to say' that the original conviction was mistaken. On 2 January 1995 the Supreme Court upheld this decision by a six to three vote and Jacobs was executed by lethal injection two days later. 'I have news for you,' he said moments before he died. 'There's not going to be an execution. This is premeditated murder.'[83]

Those campaigning to end the injustices of the death penalty, however, can expect little help from politicians in the Democratic Party, who have increasingly used support for capital punishment as a way to demonstrate that they are 'tough on crime'. 'Democrats around the country are determined never again to permit Republican candidates to capture the symbols of law and order,' says one political consultant. 'Politics is nuclear. Take no prisoners'.[84] Bill Clinton, in particular, took this advice to heart in his campaign for the presidency. During the crucial New Hampshire primary at the beginning of 1992 he returned home to Arkansas to sign the death warrant for Rickey Ray Rector, a brain damaged black man, and then boasted that, while other candidates claimed to support capital punishment, he was the only one who had enforced it.

Conclusion

Crime policy in the US has little to do with reducing crime or protecting the public, and much more to do with controlling economically deprived sections of the population, providing an ideological diversion from more serious problems, and reinforcing racial divisions within the working class. This 'law and order' agenda has been promoted by both Republicans and Democrats, and in recent years has seemed to carry all before it.

Despite this, however, the ruling class agenda on crime can be fought. Indeed, it already is being fought in a variety of ways, ranging from the work of human rights organisations to the frequent occurrence of prison riots. Yet by themselves the people engaged in these activities lack the social power to affect the system except at the margins. Such resistance can only be successful if it is linked to a much broader movement for social change. During the 1960s and early 1970s, for example, movements fighting for progressive change in the wider society sparked a radical prisoners' rights movement within US prisons. But as the outside movements went into decline the prison organisations were isolated and crushed as well.[85] Today the ruling class crime agenda can be successfully challenged by linking the fight against it to a more general working class fightback for decent jobs, education, healthcare, and other social programmes the budgets of which are being slashed due to the growth of the voracious crime industry. In the longer term such a movement has the potential power not just to oppose current policies, but to end the system responsible for the deprivation and poverty which give rise to crime in the first place.

Notes

Thanks to Joe Allen, Noam Chomsky, Ahmed Shawki and especially Eric Ruder for advice and bibliographical help.

1 J Brotman and J Treat, 'Doing Violence to Ourselves: the Omnibus Crime Bill of 1994', *RESIST Newsletter*, vol 3, no 10 (December 1994), p5.
2 Some Republicans nevertheless voted against the bill because of a gun control clause which bans a number of assault weapons.
3 I restrict my discussion in this article to political responses to 'street crime'—ie burglary, theft, assault, rape, murder and similar offences. In fact it is 'suite crime'—white collar and corporate crime (not to mention many business activities which are legal under capitalism)—which costs ordinary citizens far more in financial terms and which is responsible for many more deaths each year. How 'crime' gets defined is clearly also a political issue. See M Parenti, *Democracy for the Few*, (fifth edition, New York, 1988), pp112-121, 124-127.
4 L Selfa, 'Clinton's Crime Bill—We Need Jobs, Not More Jails', *Socialist Worker* (US), September 1994; J Brotman and J Treat, op cit.
5 N Christie, *Crime Control as Industry* (London, 1993).
6 W Chambliss, 'Policing the Ghetto Underclass: the Politics of Law and Law Enforcement', *Social Problems*, vol 41, no 2 (May 1994), p184.
7 J Brotman and J Treat, op cit, p1.
8 D Baum, 'The Drug War on Civil Liberties', *The Nation*, 29 June 1992, p886.
9 A L Shapiro, *We're Number One: Where America Stands—and Falls—in the New World Order* (New York, 1992), p138.
10 R Waters, 'No Exit', *SF Weekly*, 9 March, 1994, p11. California's population is about 31 million, China's is over 1.1 billion.
11 S Whitman, 'The Crime of Black Imprisonment', *Z Magazine* (May 1992), p69.
12 W Chambliss, op cit, pp183-184.
13 Even three strikes is too generous for some, however. A 'two strikes' law—life without parole for second time violent offenders—was approved by voters in Georgia in November 1994, and California governor Pete Wilson is now pushing a 'one strike' proposal for rapists, child molesters and arsonists.
14 *New York Times*, 3 January 1995.
15 R Waters, op cit, pp11-12.
16 W Chambliss, op cit, p181.
17 S Whitman, op cit, p69.
18 A Hacker, *Two Nations: Black and White, Separate, Hostile, Unequal* (New York, 1992), p189.
19 The high crime rate in the US is due to a variety of factors, but in particular the country's exceptionally high poverty level. See E M Schur, *Our Criminal Society: the Social and Legal Sources of Crime in America* (Englewood Cliffs, New Jersey, 1969) for a somewhat dated but nevertheless still useful discussion.
20 W Chambliss, op cit, p184.

21 J Jackson and J Naureckas, 'Crime Contradictions: US News Illustrates Flaws in Crime Coverage', *Extra!* vol 7, no 3, May/June 1994, p11.
22 D H Bayley, *Police for the Future* (New York, 1994), ch 1.
23 Quoted in S Whitman, op cit, p71.
24 P Gasper, 'The reality behind California's "Three Strikes and You're Out" law', *Socialist Worker* (US), November 4, 1994
25 P Wright, 'Three Strikes Racks 'Em Up', *Z Magazine*, June 1994, p13.
26 P Gasper, op cit.
27 P Wright, op cit, p13.
28 W Chambliss, op cit, p188.
29 *New York Times,* 23 January 1994.
30 *Washington Post National Weekly Edition*, January 9-15, 1995.
31 J Jackson and J Naureckas, op cit, p10.
32 *Los Angeles Times*, 13 February 1994. Cited in J Jackson and J Naureckas, op cit, p10.
33 W Chambliss, op cit, p191.
34 Chambliss does not put the point in terms of ruling class interests.
35 W Chambliss, op cit, p191.
36 See S Smith, 'Twilight of the American Dream', *International Socialism* 54 (Spring 1992).
37 On the role of racism see A Callinicos, *Race and Class* (London, 1993).
38 One exception was the 1928 presidential election. At a time when, as one commentator notes, 'the police routinely held suspects incommunicado for long periods and extracted confessions through physical and psychological torture, often with the prosecutor's knowledge or participation', the Republican candidate Herbert Hoover made 'law and order' an issue in his campaign. 'Every student of our law enforcement mechanism', Hoover told one audience, 'knows full well...that its procedures unduly favour the criminal...and that justice must be more swift and sure.' (C E Silberman, *Criminal Violence, Criminal Justice* [New York, 1978], p172.) He raised the issue again in his inaugural address and set up the Wickersham Commission to study the problem. When the commission found that the criminal justice system was brutal, corrupt and inefficient, however, its reports were shelved and its recommendations ignored (L M Friedman, *Crime and Punishment in American History* [New York, 1993], pp273-274).
39 Quoted in L M Friedman, op cit, p274.
40 Quoted in W Chambliss, op cit, p190.
41 Goldwater's bellicose views on foreign policy probably hurt him the most. On one memorable occasion during the campaign he suggested 'lob[bing] one into the men's room of the Kremlin.' (Quoted in D Smith and M Gebbie, *Reagan for Beginners* [New York, 1984], p74.)
42 J House (ed), *George C Wallace Tells It Like It Is* (Selma, Alabama, 1969), p29.
43 Ibid, p95.
44 Ibid, p66.
45 Ibid, p70.
46 Privately Nixon was a racist who believed that blacks are genetically inferior to whites, and an anti-Semite. See M A Genovese, *The Nixon Presidency: Power and Politics in Turbulent Times* (New York, 1990), p82, and S E Ambrose, *Nixon, Volume Two: the Triumph of a Politician 1962-1972* (New York, 1989), pp272-273, 641. After he was elected Nixon did all he could to slow down the implementation of civil rights legislation in order to shore up his support in the South (MA Genovese, op cit, pp81-88.)
47 Phillips was a Goldwater supporter who worked for Nixon's attorney general, John Mitchell, after the election.

48 S E Ambrose, op cit, p154.
49 Quoted in F Pearce, *Crimes of the Powerful: Marxism, Crime and Deviance* (London, 1976), p77.
50 S E Ambrose, op cit, p125.
51 Ibid, pp144-145.
52 Ibid, p184. Humphrey was also, of course, an enthusiastic defender of the war in Vietnam who said nothing to protest at the brutal police attacks on demonstrators outside the Democratic convention in Chicago where he was nominated. Nevertheless, his response is striking—no serious Democratic candidate would say such a thing today. In 1968, at the height of the post-war boom, the Democratic Party stood for guns and butter. Today, over a quarter of a century and three major recessions later, with the US economy mired in long term crisis, the promise of butter has long since been abandoned.
53 Ibid, p202.
54 M A Genovese, op cit, p90.
55 Ibid, p89.
56 Ibid, p88.
57 Ibid, pp89-90.
58 The function of crime policy was not, of course, purely ideological. It was during the Nixon presidency that the FBI carried out murderous attacks on members of the Black Panther Party, and in 1972 imprisonment rates began to climb for the first time in 50 years (S Whitman, op cit, p70).
59 Quotes and information in the preceding two paragraphs are from D Smith and M Gebbie, op cit, pp138-142.
60 F Barbash, 'Reagan Court Already Here', *Manchester Guardian Weekly*, 22 July 1984.
61 Ibid.
62 P Wright, op cit, p13.
63 D R Gordon, 'Cleaning Up the Mess at Justice', *The Nation*, 19 April 1993, p522.
64 *San Francisco Chronicle*, 21 April 1990.
65 J Allen, 'The "War on Drugs" in US History', *International Socialist Organization Internal Bulletin*, June 1990.
66 D Baum, op cit, p886.
67 M Davis, *City of Quartz* (New York, 1990), p290.
68 L Selfa, 'Is Bill Clinton the Lesser Evil?', *Socialist Worker* (US), September 1992.
69 L Selfa, 'Clinton's Crime Bill', op cit.
70 L Sustar, 'Black Leaders Give Clinton Liberal Cover', *Socialist Worker* (US), August 1994.
71 D Baum, op cit, p886.
72 'The Strange Death of Liberal Los Angeles', *Z Magazine*, November 1993, p50.
73 M Yates, *Longer Hours, Fewer Jobs: Employment and Unemployment in the United States* (New York, 1994), pp10-11.
74 L M Friedman, op cit, pp 316-317.
75 M Parenti, op cit, p131.
76 M Ross, 'A Matter of Life and Death', *Socialist Review* 177 (July/August 1994), p17.
77 Cited in A L Shapiro, op cit, p125.
78 Ibid.
79 L M Friedman, op cit, p319; M Ross, op cit, p18. Two years later the court ruled that the execution of the mentally impaired is also constitutional. According to an estimate made by the Southern Centre for Human Rights, at least 10 percent of those on death row lack the intellectual capacity to understand their situation. See *Manchester Guardian Weekly*, 3 May 1992; C McCarthy, 'Executing the Retarded is Legal Lynching', *Los Angeles Times*, 4 December 1992.

80 M Ross, 'The Execution of Innocence', *RESIST Newsletter*, vol 3, no 10, December 1994, p3. Ross is himself a condemned man on Connecticut's death row, currently appealing his conviction.
81 Ibid, pp4-5.
82 Ibid, p4.
83 *New York Times*, 3 January 1995. *San Francisco Examiner*, 8 January 1995.
84 *Manchester Guardian Weekly*, 22 April 1990.
85 See E Cummins, *The Rise and Fall of California's Radical Prison Movement* (Palo Alto, California, 1994).

Backward to liberalism

*A review of David Miliband, ed, **Reinventing the Left** (Polity Press) £45.00/£11.95*

ALEX CALLINICOS

British politics is in an intriguing state of flux. The crisis the Major government has been in since the pound was driven out of the Exchange Rate Mechanism on Black Wednesday, 16 September 1992, shows no sign of abating. On the contrary, the apparently endless succession of bungles and scandals at Westminster serves to reinforce a popular mood of intense hatred of the Tories. Meanwhile issues such as the revival of fascism and the Criminal Justice Act have stimulated mass movements that are bringing a new generation into radical politics.

This situation amounts to a remarkable opportunity for the British left to begin to reverse the defeats it suffered in the 1980s. And, at the level of electoral politics, it is the parliamentary left—in the shape of the Labour Party—which is the chief beneficiary of the Tories' unpopularity. Labour, in the months following Tony Blair's elevation to the party leadership in July 1994, established an astonishing lead in the opinion polls.

But what does Blair's 'New Labour'—as his advisers have rebaptised the party—stand for? In what respects do its policies constitute an alternative to those of the Tories? What hope of a better future does it offer after the terrible suffering and waste inflicted under Margaret Thatcher and John Major?

Even by the standards set by his predecessors Neil Kinnock and John Smith, Blair has been extraordinarily cautious in his response to these questions. Detailed policy commitments from 'New Labour' are still very thin on the ground. It is, therefore, useful to have some pointers provided by the essays collected together in *Reinventing the Left*. True, they were based on papers delivered mainly by left wing academics at a conference held in September 1993, before Smith's death and Blair's accession. Nevertheless, they are edited by David Miliband, by all accounts one of the key figures in the new leader's kitchen cabinet, and the contributors include Blair's close ally, the shadow chancellor of the exchequer, Gordon Brown. The whole tone of the collection and the manner in which it is packaged is intended to convey the impression that its aim is to reassess the socialist tradition for a new age. Miliband explains that: 'the essays in this book all seek to give modern relevance to old values. These values have inherent in them an ambition to change in a fundamental way advanced market societies.' At the same time, however, '[n]one of the authors of the essays in this volume believe that this project can be achieved by revolutionary upheaval, but they do believe in social and economic reform'.[1]

The contributors thus place themselves firmly within the reformist tradition. Reformism itself has, of course, various different strains. Left reformism, which seeks a fundamental restructuring of the British state and society, is honourably represented in Britain today by figures such as Tony Benn and Dennis Skinner. But they are very much part of the 'Old Labour' which the contributors to *Reinventing the Left* want to break from. Miliband and his co-thinkers want to give 'modern relevance to old values'. This has, of course, become one of the main themes of Blair's 'modernisation' of the Labour Party. Thus scrapping Clause Four of the Labour Party constitution, with its commitment to common ownership of the economy, is presented as an 'updating' which will leave Labour's 'values' untouched. This kind of argument has been used before. Back in the 1970s, I remember, the *Daily Telegraph* used the advertising slogan 'Times Change. Values Don't.' Tony Blair's message to the Labour rank and file seems to be the same. But what exactly are the values which he—and the contributors to *Reinventing the Left*—are seeking to preserve and indeed reinvigorate?

The answer is implicit in former *New Left Review* editor Perry Anderson's comment on the sociologist Tony Giddens's opening essay. (The collection is organised around a series of major papers, each appended with a brief comment. It is generally, though not always, true that the comments are considerably better—more incisive, more realistic and at any rate shorter—than the essays to which they respond.) Anderson picks up on Giddens's claim that we are witnessing at present 'the exhaustion of received political ideologies', notably of both liberalism and socialism.[2] He protests:

The reality is that the liberalism which claims victory over socialism today is at the zenith of its self confidence; it numbers more adherents across the world than any time this century. It is a mistake for the Left to comfort itself by thinking otherwise.[3]

There is an obvious objection to this assertion. The wave of euphoria which followed the 1989 revolutions in Eastern Europe was rapidly dissipated as a series of developments demonstrated the inability of liberal capitalism to organise the world on a peaceful and stable basis—the Gulf War, the chaos in the former Soviet Union, the carnage in Bosnia, the global recession of the early 1990s, the economic collapse of most of the Stalinist succession states. Hence the widespread scepticism with which Francis Fukuyama's announcement of the end of history and the definitive triumph of economic and political liberalism was greeted, even on the right.

Nevertheless, Anderson is right in the sense that the influence of liberalism as an *ideology* probably is at its 20th century 'zenith'. The 1989 revolutions brought to a climax the long process through which Stalinism and social democracy—the two dominant traditions on the left since the 1920s—had been gradually discredited. The associated decline of Keynesian economics—along with cruder pressures, such as the structural adjustment programmes imposed by the International Monetary Fund and the World Bank—helped to create a vogue for free market economics throughout the Third World. The result is an intellectual climate in which no alternative to liberalism is considered to be credible.

The resulting cultural sea change is very striking particularly on the academic left, where the flight away from Marxism has assumed lemming like proportions in recent years. Often this retreat into liberalism is obscured by the adoption of some variant or other of postmodernism, where grandiloquent philosophical rhetoric helps conceal a timid acceptance of the status quo. Sometimes, however, the endorsement of liberalism is more or less explicit. *Reinventing the Left* is an example of this latter tendency.

Thus Miliband argues that:

the Left's traditional emphasis on the value of equality and solidarity needs to be supplemented by renewed commitment to the extension of personal autonomy in an increasingly interdependent world. The Right has made hay by arguing that equality means uniformity, but it is the development of a coherent understanding of the relationship between equality and diversity that is attempted here.[4]

There are, in fact, few signs of such a 'coherent understanding' emerging in *Reinventing the Left.*[5] David Held does offer the following 'principle of autonomy':

> *persons should enjoy equal rights (and, accordingly, equal obligations) in the framework which generates and limits the opportunities available to them; that is, they should be free and equal in the determination of the conditions of their own lives, so long as they do not deploy this framework to negate the rights of others.*[6]

This new 'principle' has a familiar ring. It seems, in fact, to be nothing but a restatement, couched in the language of rights, of John Stuart Mill's famous pronouncement in *On Liberty*: 'The only freedom which deserves the name is that of pursuing our own good in our own way, so long as we do not attempt to deprive others of theirs or impede their efforts to obtain it.'[7] The standard socialist objection to this classic definition of modern liberalism has, of course, always been that most people's equal right to freedom is nullified, or at least gravely qualified, by their lack of access to the productive resources required to support themselves. They are thus not 'free and equal in the determination of the conditions of their own lives'.

Held is aware of this objection. His principle of autonomy proscribes what he (somewhat bizarrely) calls 'nautonomy', ie '*the assymetrical production and distribution of life-chances which limits and erodes the possibilities of political participation.*' It follows that:

> *If people's equal interest in the principle of autonomy is to be protected, extensive redistribution of goods and services may be required in order to ensure that people who have been handicapped, through nautonomic* [sic] *circumstances and/or unequal endowment, receive those resources needed to further their status as equally free within the process of self determination.*[8]

Talk of redistribution immediately raises the question of the market. One doesn't have to be a Marxist to recognise that a market economy generates systematic inequalities of resources and income, and thus what Held calls 'nautonomy'. Thus Will Hutton of the *Guardian* notes:

> *The operation of markets and deregulated capitalism has reproduced in our times the forces of 100 years ago. Absolute living standards may be higher, but the same stark inequalities are emerging, and in relative terms exceed the degree of inequality then.*[9]

Redistribution to give people genuine control of their lives therefore inevitably involves interference in the market. But what does this imply? Miliband asserts on behalf of his contributors, 'The role of politics is not to abolish markets, but to organise and regulate them.'[10] To properly understand the equivocal answers *Reinventing the Left* gives to this question it may be helpful briefly to consider the historical relationship between liberalism and Labourism in Britain.

There are different economic programmes consistent with the basic conception of individual freedom expounded by Mill. The *laissez faire* liberalism politically rehabilitated in the 1980s by Ronald Reagan and Margaret Thatcher asserts that if the market is left to its own devices, with the economic activities of the state reduced to the lowest possible level, human welfare will be maximised. Other liberals, however, including Mill, have denied this, and insisted some degree of state interference is necessary to offset the injustices and inefficiencies generated by the unrestrained market.

The emergence of Labour after the First World War as the main electoral rival to the Tories saw an influx into the party of supporters of this variant of liberalism. Many ex-Liberals came more or less reluctantly to the conclusion that Labour was the only effective vehicle for the New Liberalism of social reform devised by Gladstone in the late 19th century and implemented by the triumphant Campbell-Bannerman and Asquith administrations in the years before 1914.

However, the chief architect of this synthesis of liberalism and social democracy never joined the Labour Party. John Maynard Keynes developed a critique of *laissez faire*, showing that the unrestrained market would lead precisely to the kind of chronic mass unemployment characteristic of the inter-war years. He argued that the state could, by judicious adjustments to taxation and public spending, ensure that the economy avoided the sharp fluctuations of boom and slump, and thereby secure full employment. He thus provided social democracy with an economic programme which offered an alternative to the unbridled market but avoided any direct confrontation with the structures of capitalist economic power. Though Keynes remained a Liberal, young Labour intellectuals such as Douglas Jay and Hugh Gaitksell proselytised for his ideas in the 1930s. During the long boom of the 1950s and 1960s Keynesian economics was adapted by leading 'revisionists' such as Anthony Crosland and John Strachey, and gave right wing social democracy its intellectual underpinnings.[11]

The return of economic crisis in the late 1960s—particularly in its initial form of 'stagflation', which combined accelerating inflation and mass unemployment—discredited the Keynesian methods of demand management which had previously been held responsible for the post-war boom. The crisis set the stage for the revival of the free market liberalism advocated by Milton Friedman and Friedrich von Hayek. Developments over the past 25 years—in particular the pronounced tendency to the greater global integration of capital—have, by reducing the ability of states to manage their 'national' economies' further weakened the main instrument of Keynesian policies. What Nigel Harris has called 'the end of capitalism in one country' seemed also to sound the death knell of interventionist liberalism.[13]

Where, then, does this leave social democracy? What does 'regulating' the market mean in the post-Keynesian era? *Reinventing the Left* offers a hubbub of different answers, some mutually inconsistent, none of them convincing. In some cases we are presented with nothing but muddle. Giddens, for example, attacks what he calls the '"cybernetic model" of social life' traditionally accepted by the left, according to which 'a system (in the case of socialism, the economy) can best be organised by being subordinated to a directive intelligence (the state, understood in one form or another)'. This form of organisation can't work, he claims, in a system as complex as a modern economy. This argument is strongly reminiscent of Hayek's attempt to prove the impossibility of any form of socialist planning, and therefore the necessity of leaving the market to its own devices. But Giddens refuses to draw the latter conclusion, arguing instead that '[u]nchecked capitalist markets still have many of the unhappy results to which socialists have long pointed'. Well then, how are these results to be avoided? Presumably, *laissez faire* won't do. But with what is it to be replaced? Beyond reaffirming his rejection of 'the cybernetic model of socialism', Giddens doesn't say.[14]

Other contributors are more up front. French Socialist Party leader Michel Rocard, for example, opts for '[a] society of social solidarity in a market economy', with the emphasis on the latter. Thus he argues that the left has:

> *underestimated the power of competition. Competition is the definition of existence in the modern era. Human life is made of competition. How can we imagine an economy which would not have competition as its first element?*[15]

Many socialists would be unwilling to take lessons from a former prime minister in François Mitterrand's disastrous administration. And indeed Will Hutton takes him to task for having 'yielded too much ground. The notion that markets are the only successful form of organisation...requires more caution.' He goes on to point out that 'there are many forms of market and capitalism, with varying degrees of efficiency and social cohesion; the Left must discriminate between them'.[16]

The thought is that, rather than offer a global alternative to capitalism as a system, the left should espouse that variant of capitalism which offers the best chance of realising their objectives. Thus, in the *Ten Commandments for Social Democrats* with which the book concludes, James Cornford and Patricia Hewitt invite the reader to 'decide what kind of capitalist you are'.[17]

This stress on the varieties of capitalism has been made fashionable in social democratic circles by a recent book by the French businessman and journalist Michel Albert. Albert argues that the collapse of Stalinism has indeed marked the triumph of capitalism. This does not, however, as Fukuyama claims, amount to the end of history. On the contrary, a new conflict is now beginning to occupy the centre stage of world history, that between the two main models of capitalism prevalent in the developed economies.

The first, 'Anglo-American capitalism', comes closer to the requirements of *laissez-faire* liberalism. The market is increasingly unregulated, individuals are left to pursue their own destiny, and poverty and inequality are growing. Confronting it is the 'Rhine model' of capitalism, most fully developed in West Germany but to some extent to be found throughout the European Union. Here the market is closely regulated, networks of social co-operation bind together industry, finance and the state on the one hand, and capital and labour on the other. High levels of welfare spending ensure social cohesion and reduce inequality. Albert believes that Rhine capitalism represents a more efficient and humane version of the market and therefore will be able to see off the Anglo-American challenge.[18]

Albert's analysis informs many of the contributions to *Reinventing the Left*. Rocard, for example, argues that 'we have a civilisation contest' and argues that the EU should actively seek to export its combination of 'human rights and social protection'[19] (rights and protection denied to many blacks and Arabs in France during his premiership). Some contributors go beyond this very dubious sloganeering, advocating what Miliband calls 'an egalitarian productivism'.[20] This idea is most carefully developed by Joel Rogers and Wolfgang Streeck. They argue that 'the Left must again save capitalism from itself'. In the 1930s Keynes' principle of effective demand offered a way of getting capitalism out of the Great Depression: higher public spending would stimulate demand and therefore generate an increase in output and employment. This restored growth and profits and made possible higher living standards and the development of the welfare state: both labour and capital benefited from the Keynesian remedy.[21]

The contemporary equivalent of Keynesian effective demand, Rogers and Streeck argue, is what they call '*effective supply*'. The economic transformations of the past quarter century have left capitalism much more flexible, but also much more disorganised than it was in the recent past. It needs a higher level of social co-operation and co-ordination, one that the market cannot provide. In particular, high productivity, high wage capitalism requires a whole range of 'public goods' such as training which no individual firm has an interest in producing because this would raise costs and reduce profits. Such public goods would however benefit capitalists and workers alike if the state were to supply them. Indeed, on this strategy, 'equality and democratic participation' become 'a source of productive progress'.[22] Rather than confront the traditional reformist dilemma that greater social justice will undermine the operation of the market economy, the left can have its cake and eat it.

Gordon Brown offers a cruder version of the same argument in his contribution.[23] As Robert Kuttner makes clear in a highly effective critique, it assumes a rose hued view of capitalism's future course. Thus:

> *Many new jobs require workers with only minimal skills. Moreover, even higher-order skills do not necessarily imply empowerment or durable worker/employer relationships. According to Manpower Inc, which is now the largest employer in the US, semi-skilled computer operators who know graphics programmes are now the fastest growing category of temporary workers, and such workers can be trained in a week.*[24]

Moreover, Kuttner points out, whether higher productivity benefits workers depends upon the overall state of the economy: 'To assure that productivity gains in one factory add up to gains in living standards for workers rather than technological unemployment requires a macroeconomic context of high growth and full employment.' Rogers' and Streek's supply side reformism must therefore confront the problem of insufficient demand—and more generally capitalism's tendency to boom and slump—which Keynes's economics, for all its faults, sought to address.[25]

Finally, 'egalitarian productivism' ignores the question of power, and the class conflicts from which it is inseparable. Whatever benefits capital might gain from higher state spending on such things as the provision of training, Kuttner suggests:

> *most employers (at least in the Anglo-Saxon countries) would rather suffer the inefficiencies than tolerate the increased power of the state and the labour movement that an alternative policy regime would entail. The Clinton administration is baffled and dismayed that even though its proposed health legislation would save most large corporations significant costs in the form of reduced or capped health insurance premiums, few large companies support*

the plan because they resist an expansion of the reach of the state.[26]

The naive optimism uncovered by Kuttner is symptomatic. Thus no contributor notices that the early 1990s have seen 'Rhine capitalism' thrown into crisis in its west German heartland by the combined impact of unification and recession. The uneasy recovery of the mid-1990s is unlikely to involve much abatement of the competitive pressures on the European economies to continue the process of restructuring, and therefore to undermine the systems of social protection supposedly distinctive to the 'Rhine model'.[27] The contributors to *Reinventing the Left* are in danger of exaggerating the differences between variants of capitalism that may be coming to resemble each other much more closely.

Our new social democrats are therefore unable to come up with a clear and plausible account of their alternative to capitalism as it exists today. What, then, does this suggest about the politics of 'New Labour'? All the signs are that the leadership's commitment to a 'dynamic market economy'—a phrase repeated by Blair and Brown like a mantra—overrides all others. The search for something fairer and more rational than the market—expressed, for example, in Clause Four, and pursued even by Keynes and those influenced by him—is being definitively abandoned by the new Labour leadership.

All that is left to distinguish Labour from the Tories is its 'values'. Chief among these is that of 'community', another 'New Labour' buzzword. Brown, for example, argues that 'modern socialism' is distinguished by the belief that 'the wellbeing of the individual is best understood within the context of the broader community'.[28] The vagueness and ambiguity characteristic of much 'New Labour' thinking are especially dangerous here. For there is nothing necessarily progressive about appeals to 'community'. It depends on the nature of the community concerned, and, in particular, where the boundaries are set which determine who is included and who excluded from that community. For example, the slogan, 'Island homes for Island people', raised during the council by-election on the Isle of Dogs in September 1993 was, in effect, a racist one, since it tacitly defined the Island 'community' in a way that excluded blacks.

'Communitarianism', developed by philosophers critical of liberal individualism such as Alasdair MacIntyre and Michael Walzer, is thus no real alternative.[29] In Labour's case invocation of the value of 'community' does not provide any justification for making any inroads into the market, since 'values' are, to all intents and purposes, segregated from actual policies. It has instead helped to legitimise Blair's attempts to steal the Tories' clothes on such issues as law and order and the family. This is a mug's game, since Labour's roots in the organised working class movement are likely to prevent it from ever going as far as the Tories can in stirring up reactionary sentiments around issues such as crime and race in order to win votes.

Nevertheless the extent to which nice 'New Labour' and nasty old Tories converge, even at the level of rhetoric, is very striking. Consider for example, Gordon Brown's advocacy of 'an enabling state offering new pathways out of poverty for people trapped in welfare, showing that the true role of government is to foster personal responsibility and not to substitute for it. The welfare state should not just be a safety net but a springboard'.[30] Cornford and Hewitt repeat the same metaphor in their *Ten Commandments*, instructing social democrats to 'build trampolines, not safety nets'.[31]

At much the same time as I read these words in the autumn of 1994, Tory social security secretary Peter Lilley could be heard using precisely the same formulation to justify his latest attack on the welfare state. Of course, there is nothing politicians converge on more quickly than cliches. But much more significant than the use of the same words is the ideas they share: 'New Labour' has come increasingly to accept the New Right critique of the welfare state, namely that it deprives people of the incentive to work and imprisons them in a 'culture of dependency'.

Cornford's and Hewitt's Second Commandment is to 'think big'.[32] Yet nothing is more remarkable about *Reinventing the Left* than the narrowness of its horizons and the poverty of imagination most of the contributions display. A further retreat from the objective of a radical transformation of society is dressed up as 'new thinking'.

And this points to a paradox. If one reflects on the condition of humankind as the second millennium AD draws to a close, then it is hard not to conclude that some kind of global revolution is necessary. This conclusion doesn't have to be deduced from Marxist first principles, but can be arrived at by considering the various afflictions from which humanity suffers—widespread mass unemployment, endemic poverty in much of the Third World, the continuing proliferation of devastatingly effective military technologies, the progressive destruction of the environment. Addressing these problems requires a drastic reordering of the priorities on which the world is currently organised, and that in turn depends on radically changing the structure of power and privilege on a world scale—global revolution, in other words.[33]

Yet, although revolution is more urgently needed now even than in the past, it is an objective that much of the left intelligentsia no longer regard as either feasible or desirable. This is not the place to examine the reasons for this collective loss of nerve: suffice it to say the collapse of Stalinism helped solidify among many left wing intellectuals the belief that there is no alternative to the rampant market.[34] If nothing else, *Reinventing the Left* serves to highlight how practically confining the implications of holding this belief are. Within the constraints it imposes there seems to be nothing to do but pursue the same policies as the right, only with a (somewhat) different rhetoric.

I have called this review 'Backward to Liberalism', parodying the title of a famous book by the poet Stephen Spender, *Foreward from Liberalism*, which described his (as it turned out) brief flirtation with Communism in the mid-1930s. But putting it like this is, in some ways, unfair to liberalism. For Marxism and liberalism are not completely at odds.[35] Liberalism, after all, is the product of the age of the great bourgeois revolutions—England 1640, America 1776, France 1789. Liberalism, indeed, can carry a revolutionary charge, and not simply because it emerged from the struggle to break down the barriers imposed on individual freedom by absolutism. The ideals it evokes—life, liberty, and the pursuit of happiness, *liberté, égalité, fraternité*—are only capable of fully being realised in a society where capitalist exploitation and the oppressions with which it is bound up have been abolished.[36] The promise of liberalism can only be fulfilled by being radicalised. Seeking to confine socialism within the limits of liberalism, as most contributors to *Reinventing the Left* do, amounts to a betrayal of both traditions.

This will not prevent most of those seeking change in Britain today from looking towards the Labour Party in any electoral contest. Anyone who wants to get rid of the Tories has no choice but to vote for 'New Labour' at the ballot box. But if they wish also to scrap the society which both produced Thatcherism and was strengthened by it, they must look elsewhere.

Notes

1 D Miliband (ed), 'Introduction', to *Reinventing the Left* (Cambridge, 1994), hereinafter *RL*, p15.
2 A Giddens, 'Brave New World', in *RL*, p27.
3 P Anderson, 'Power, Politics and the Enlightenment', in *RL*, p41.
4 D Miliband, 'Introduction', in *RL*, p6.
5 Some interesting points are made on the issues of race, ethnicity, and religion by T Modood, 'Ethnic Difference and Racial Equality', and B Parekh, 'Minority Rights, Majority Values', but their arguments are developed to a large degree independently of the book's main themes.
6 D Held, 'Inequalities of Power, Problems of Democracy', in *RL*, p48.
7 J S Mill, *On Liberty* (Harmondsworth, 1974), p72.
8 D Held, 'Inequalities', pp49, 57. Held's argument may hold up better in the forthcoming book from which his paper is drawn.
9 W Hutton, 'The Social Market in a Global Context', in *RL*, p162.
10 D Miliband, 'Introduction', in *RL*, p6.
11 P Clarke, *Liberals and Social Democrats* (Cambridge, 1978), P Williams, *Hugh Gaitskell* (London, 1979), and R Skidelsky, *John Maynard Keynes*, II (London, 1992).

12 See C Harman, *Explaining the Crisis* (London, 1984), ch 3.
13 N Harris, *Of Bread and Guns* (Harmondsworth, 1983), pp229ff. For a full analysis of the implications of what has come to be called 'globalisation' see C Harman, 'The State and Capitalism Today', *International Socialism* 51 (1991).
14 A Giddens, 'Brave New world', pp25, 28. See F A von Hayek (ed), *Collectivist Economic Planning* (London, 1935).
15 M Rocard, 'Social Solidarity in a Mixed Economy', in *RL*, p153.
16 W Hutton, 'Social Market', p159.
17 J Cornford and P Hewitt. 'Dos and Don'ts for Social Democrats', in *RL*, p252.
18 M Albert, *Capitalism against Capitalism* (London, 1993).
19 M Rocard, 'Social Solidarity', in *RL*, p157.
20 D Miliband, 'Introduction', in *RL*, p20.
21 J Rogers and W Streeck, 'Productive Solidarities', in *RL*, p133.
22 Ibid, pp135, 138.
23 G Brown, 'The Politics of Potential', in *RL*.
24 R Kuttner, 'Don't Forget the Demand Side', in *RL*, p149.
25 Ibid, p149.
26 Ibid, pp149-150. Anderson also highlights the realities of social conflict ignored by other contributors: 'Power', pp41-43.
27 See A Callinicos, 'Crisis and Class Struggle in Europe Today', *International Socialism* 63 (1994).
28 Brown, 'Politics', p118.
29 A MacIntyre, *After Virtue* (London, 1981), and M Walzer, *Sphere of Justice* (Oxford, 1983).
30 Brown, 'Politics', p114.
31 Cornford and Hewitt, 'Do's and Don'ts', in *RL*, p253.
32 Ibid, p251.
33 It is, therefore, not surprising that it should be one of the papers on the environment that complains that 'social democracy, originally a creed to conquer capitalism, now uncritically accepts its assumptions', S Tindale, 'Sustaining Social Democracy', in *RL*, p205.
34 Eric Hobsbawm's deeply disappointing *Age of Extremes* (London, 1994) is a striking example of this kind of pessimistic world view.
35 For a good discussion of the assumptions shared by Marxism and liberalism, see W Kymlicka, *Liberalism, Community, and Culture* (Oxford, 1989), ch 6.
36 See especially E Balibar, '"Droits de l'homme" et "droits du citoyen"', *Actuel Marx*, 8 (1990). Jacques Bidet uses Balibar's argument to give a radical interpretation of the theory of justice developed by the leading American left liberal philosopher John Rawls: *Théorie de la Modernité* (Paris, 1990), ppl19ff.

Matewan: film and working class struggle

JOHN NEWSINGER

On 19 May 1920 a party of 12 Baldwin-Felts private detectives led by Albert and Lee Felts arrived in the small town of Matewan, West Virginia. They had been busy evicting the families of striking miners from company housing on behalf of the Stone Mountain Coal Company and were now on their way back to the Baldwin-Felts headquarters in Bluefield. Their presence in Matewan was deliberately provocative. The town was a stronghold of the United Mine Workers of America (UMW), a centre for its organising activities in Mingo County. Only a fortnight earlier the union had held a rally attended by over 3,000 miners, black and white, in the town. Now an armed confrontation was to take place on the main street between the Baldwin-Felts men and Matewan's mayor, Cabell Testerman, and chief of police, Sid Hatfield, both former miners and staunch UMW supporters. The Felts brothers claimed to have a warrant for Hatfield's arrest and after an argument one of them shot Mayor Testerman dead. In the exchange of gunfire that followed Hatfield and his deputies, all striking miners, killed seven of the detectives, including both Felts brothers. Two striking miners, Robert Mullins and Tot Tinsley, were killed.[1]

This gunfight was celebrated as a great victory by the UMW in West Virginia and led to a dramatic increase in membership. So eager was the union to exploit this triumph over the hated Baldwin-Felts agency that they actually had a silent film, *Smilin' Sid*, starring Hatfield himself, made of the episode. The film was shown to enthusiastic, cheering miners throughout the West Virginia coalfield.[2] Over 60 years later, in 1987, the gunfight was to be the subject of another film, *Matewan*, written and directed by the radical independent film maker, John Sayles.

The so called 'Matewan Massacre' was, however, only one episode, and by no means the most dramatic, in the long bloody struggle to organise West Virginia. This particular phase, immediately after the First World War, was to culminate in the march on company controlled Logan County by over 15,000 armed miners and in the week long battle for Blair Mountain which only came to an end with the intervention of federal troops. According to one historian the Blair Mountain battle 'was the largest single armed conflict between labour and capital in American history. In this confrontation blacks and whites fought side by side for a common cause'.[3]

This article hopes to achieve two objectives: first of all to discuss the Sayles' film, both its strengths and its weaknesses, and second to examine the UMW's great historic attempt to organise the West Virginia coalfield in this period. Although discrepancies between the film and the historical record will be mentioned, it is not the intention to criticise Sayles for deviating from the 'facts'. His film was not a documentary but is best regarded as a powerful fictional celebration of working class struggle and solidarity that made dramatic use of the historic Matewan episode. It has to be judged in these terms. At the same time it will also be argued here that the UMW's defeat in West Virginia was one of the decisive struggles in post First World War America. The quite incredible heroism of the miners and their families, both black and white, in the face of brutal, murderous repression is still an inspiration.

John Sayles, radical film maker

John Sayles is without doubt the most important radical film maker at work in the United States today. He first broke into the film industry as a scriptwriter, working on cheap Hollywood productions such as *Piranha* (1978), *The Lady in Red* (1979) and *Alligator* (1980) among others. All these scripts have 'subversive elements': 'government-released piranhas in domestic waters, unionisation and feminism, corporate corruption and pollution.' According to Sayles himself, his original idea for *Alligator* was to have the monster that emerges from the Milwaukee sewers eat 'its way through the socio-economic system'.[4] His earnings from scriptwriting financed his own early films (his first film cost $60,000 to make and his second $300,000), but since then he has been able to raise more substantial sums: *Matewan*, for example, cost $4 million to make. Since his first film, *The Return of the Secaucus Seven* in 1979, Sayles has written and directed another seven films: *Lianna* (1982), *Baby, It's You* (1982), *The Brother*

From Another Planet (1984), *Matewan* (1987), *Eight Men Out* (1988), *City of Hope* (1991) and *Passion Fish* (1992). At the time of writing, another film—*The Secret of Roan Irish*—is in post-production. He has also directed a number of rock videos for Bruce Springsteen and wrote and produced the American TV series *Shannon's Deal*. Sayles is also an accomplished novelist and short story writer. His best novel is the outstanding *Union Dues*, first published in 1977, but more recently he has published a controversial anti-Castro novel, *Los Gusanos* (1991).[5]

Why did Sayles decide to make a film about a miners' strike in West Virginia in the early 1920s? He gives his reasons in the book that he wrote about the making of *Matewan*, *Thinking In Pictures*:

> *In the late sixties I hitchhiked through the area several times and most of the people who gave me rides were coal miners or people with mining in their families. They spoke with a mixture of pride and resignation about the mining—resignation about how dark and dirty and cold and wet and dangerous it was and pride that they were the people to do it, to do it well. The United Mine Workers were going through heavy times then. Their president, Tony Boyle, was accused of having his election opponent, Jock Yablonski, murdered. The coal companies and most of the political machinery that fed on them and even the UMW hierarchy denied even the existence of black lung disease and refused any compensation for it. All this was added to the usual mine accidents and disasters and wild fluctuations in coal prices. But every miner I talked to would shake his head and say, 'Buddy, this ain't nothin' compared to what used to go on. I could tell you some stories'. The stories would be about their grandfathers and uncles and fathers and mothers, and the older men would tell their own stories from when they were young.*

He goes on:

> *If storytelling has a positive function it's to put us in touch with other people's lives, to help us connect and draw strength or knowledge from people we'll never meet, to help us see beyond our own experience. The people I read about in the history books and the people I met in the hills of Kentucky and West Virginia had important stories to tell and I wanted to pass them on.*[6]

Matewan the film

Matewan tells the story of an incident in the struggle to unionise Mingo County in the West Virginia coalfield. The film begins underground with a coalface being blown. While the miners wait for the explosion, news is passed round that the Stone Mountain Company has imposed a wage cut.

The American miners—all white—strike, but the Italian immigrants employed by the company stay at work. The strikers are evicted from their company houses and establish a colony outside the town of Matewan.

Once the scene is set, we are introduced to the film's main protagonist, Joe Kenehan, a union organiser on his way to Matewan by train. Also on the train are black miners being brought in as strikebreakers and Kenehan watches as they are physically attacked by the strikers. Kenehan's first successful intervention in the conflict is to persuade the strikers that the way to defeat the company is to ally with the black and Italian miners rather than trying to drive them out. Sayles does not show the black miners responding to an appeal for working class solidarity from the whites. Instead Kenehan challenges the racism of the white miners and succeeds in persuading them to accept the appeal for working class solidarity made by the black miners who were unaware that a strike was in progress and make it clear that they are not scabs. His strategy works, and in a dramatic scene both the Italian and the black miners join the strike under the guns of the company guards.

Kenehan preaches a doctrine of working class solidarity and consistently argues against recourse to force. The strikers, he insists, must not allow themselves to be goaded into violence, no matter what the provocation. Instead they have to rely on their unity to bring them victory.

Much of the film deals with the conflict between the company spy and agent provocateur, C E Lively, who advocates the dynamiting of company property and armed attacks on the company guards, and Kenehan, who continues to urge restraint. Lively nearly succeeds in framing Kenehan as a spy, but is himself unmasked and forced to flee for his life. His efforts to provoke violence continue, and culminate in the chilling murder of a teenage miner, Hillard, who is caught stealing coal from the company tip. This killing is one of the causes of the climactic gunfight in *Matewan*.

Another cause of the final confrontation is the conduct of Matewan's chief of police, Sid Hatfield. Much to Kenehan's amazement, he does not side with the company. Although he is not shown as a union man, Hatfield nevertheless protects the rights of the miners against the company gun thugs. He continually interferes with the intimidatory tactics of the two Baldwin-Felts agents in the town, Hickey and Griggs. The decision is taken to eliminate him.

The gunfight on the main street of Matewan ends with the Baldwin-Felts agents either dead or driven off, but this victory is marred by the death of Joe Kenehan. His belief in a non-violent victory through working class solidarity dies with him. Although the film ends here, the narrator, the young miner Danny, tells of how the union went down to a violent defeat as Kenehan had foretold, but reaffirms his own commitment to the union cause.

Sayles quite deliberately decided to make Kenehan a pacifist. His intention was to give the film a parable quality, a moral dimension that questioned both the use of violence to win the strike and the viability of pacifism when confronted by the Baldwin-Felts agents. The first decision he made in writing the script:

> *...was not just to pick a side and then root for that side to be left standing when the smoke cleared, but to question the violence itself, to question it politically, strategically, morally... To bring the questioning of this violence to the foreground I made the fictional protagonist of the story, the union organiser Joe Kenehan, a pacifist. Not a reformed gunslinger who pulls his holster and guns off the wall in the last reel to wipe out the bad guys and thrill the audience, but a real pacifist, a guy who does not kill people no matter what. A guy trying to preach turning the other cheek in the land of an eye for an eye. And in having Joe question violence, pacifism is also questioned.*

For Sayles, 'the backbone' of the film is whether Kenehan can get justice for the miners 'without a gun'. There are other questions, issues and themes in the film but 'that is the spine you have to keep coming back to, the central question that drives the plot'.[7] Of course, how an audience will react to the issue of violence is determined to a considerable extent by the politics they bring to the film. A liberal audience, for example, would regard both company and union violence as equally appalling, while a revolutionary socialist audience would regret that the miners weren't better armed and that some of the Baldwin-Felts agents got away. Nevertheless the film does make it absolutely clear that, whatever Kenehan's beliefs, his own survival is in fact dependent on other men having guns and being prepared to use them, on Hatfield, on the striking miners and, on one occasion, on the intervention of the hill people. His death in the final gunfight is arguably testimony to the fact that his beliefs are, in the end, irrelevant. Once again, however, one's view derive from one's politics.

Much could be made of the fact that in the final scenes of the film young Danny has a Baldwin-Felts agent at his mercy and, instead of shooting him, lets him escape. This apparent endorsement of Kenehan's pacifism has to be balanced against the fact that Danny's mother, Elma, has just shot and killed Hickey, another Baldwin-Felts agent. The man Danny could not bring himself to shoot was unarmed and running for his life. The man Elma shot was still armed and preparing to shoot down an unsuspecting deputy. Danny's act of mercy was only made possible because Hatfield and his deputies had already shot it out with the

Baldwin-Felts agents and won. The test of pacifism is not sparing the unarmed agent but sparing Hickey and accepting the consequences that would have followed. At the very least, however, the film succeeds in raising important issues for thought and discussion.

One other point worth making here is that the whole question of pacifism which Sayles makes the backbone of the film would in fact have been altogether incomprehensible to the miners struggling to build the union in West Virginia in 1920. In circumstances where activists and organisers were routinely beaten and killed by company guards and private detectives, the readiness and ability to defend oneself was essential for survival. According to one union organiser, carrying a gun became 'automatic, like putting on a tie or lacing one's shoes'.[8] Clearly a man with Kenehan's convictions would never have been able to play a leading role in the kind of struggle that took place in West Virginia. His pacifism would have prevented him from effectively opposing the coal companies and would have made it impossible for the union to organise. Only the fact that the striking miners were armed prevented the coal companies driving them back to work at gunpoint. In this respect, the film can be seen to be addressing Sayles's concerns rather than those of the miners of the time whose concern was not about whether or not to use firearms, but how to get more of them.

It is worth briefly noting here a number of other ways in which Sayles has adapted the historical record for dramatic purposes. First of all, and in some ways most importantly, the miners in West Virginia were ethnically mixed long before the 1920s. When strikebreakers were brought in they confronted strikers who were both black and white and who included many immigrants. Sayles dramatises to good effect the achievement of black and white unity against the bosses whereas in fact this was not an issue in the West Virginia coalfield at this time. A related point is that the leader of the black miners, 'Few Clothes' Don Chain, marvellously played by James Earl Jones, was a historic figure, but in the earlier 1912-1913 strike, not in the post-war conflict.

Joe Kenehan is, of course, a fictional character, but more to the point is the fact that outside organisers did not play a leading role in the conflict which was locally led by men like Frank Keeney, Fred Mooney, Frank Ingham, Bill Blizzard and Sid Hatfield. Hatfield's role in particular was crucial: far from being an even handed mediator enforcing the law, he was an active UMW supporter, a key figure in the union's early successes in Mingo County and tremendously popular with the rank and file miners. Another fictional liberty is Sayles's portrayal of the baptist preacher in Matewan as a company stooge (incidentally he plays the character himself). This was indeed the case in company towns, but not in Matewan, an independent town with elected officials, where the baptist church served as a union meeting place. Unfortunately C E Lively was a historic figure.

One critic of *Matewan*, Stephen Brier, has argued that the film:

lacks any sense of capitalism as a system, or of individual capitalists as human agents. Many of the actual coal operators—Justus Collins and W P Tams are but two examples—lived in the area in new baronial splendour, dominating the official culture and politics of the region for nearly half a century. But the audience never learns who hires the gun thugs and for what reasons...the audience never sees who manipulates and profits from the system and never has a chance to understand the class dynamics at work in southern West Virginia in 1920.

There does seem some validity to this particular criticism, but Sayles chooses to focus on developments within the ranks of the strikers, on the community they establish. Brier goes on to criticise the film for neglecting the aftermath of the Matewan episode, for not having more to say about the march on Logan County and the battle for Blair Mountain.[9] Certainly the story is incredible enough for any number of films, with armed miners hijacking trains, company aircraft bombing the tent colonies and an army of over 15,000 workers trying to fight their way into Logan County with the express intention of hanging the sheriff, Don Chafin. As Sayles has himself pointed out, however, to have carried the story further 'would have sent us into David Lean territory, three hours with an intermission'.[10] The finance necessary for such a project could only have been raised at the cost of surrendering his control over the film which would inevitably have had an effect on its politics.

Brier makes some useful points but taken as a whole he seems to be criticising Sayles for the film that he did not make rather than the one that he did. Instead *Matewan* has to be welcomed as a celebration of working class solidarity and struggle made at the height of the Reagan-Bush era. A number of US video chains refused to carry *Matewan*. What higher praise could there be?

Class war in West Virginia

It is important not to regard the miners' struggle in West Virginia as some sort of backwoods conflict that, no matter how terrible the circumstances, had no direct relevance to the American capitalist class or to the American labour movement. This was not the case. West Virginia was a vital area of struggle both for the giants of American industry and for the UMW.

The UMW had been established in 1890 by a merger of the Knights of Labour District Assembly No 135 and the National Union of Miners and Mine Labourers. Previous attempts at union organisation had ended in often bloody defeat, but in July 1897 the UMW with only 10,000 members called a strike in the bituminous or soft coal mines across America that brought out 150,000 miners. This resulted in January 1898 in the establishment of the Central Competitive Field. The soft coal mine companies in Indiana, Illinois, Ohio and Pennsylvania were forced to accept a 'landmark' agreement that conceded 'the eight-hour day, a standard wage for men who worked on a daily basis, and a standard tonnage rate with local wage differentials'.[11] The Central Competitive Field agreement was, according to David Montgomery, 'the foundation of the UMWA's accomplishments', but, as he goes on to insist, 'almost from the day the 1898 trade agreement was signed it suffered erosion at the geographic frontiers of the CCF. Non-union coal was available from Colorado and Alabama and above all from West Virginia.'[12]

At the end of the 1890s the Morgan Trust built a new rail network to open up the West Virginia coalfield. This led to a massive expansion of the industry: in 1867 West Virginia produced 489,000 tons of coal, in 1887 it produced 4,882,000 tons and in 1917 it produced 89,384,000 tons. This flow of cheap non-union coal put the Central Competitive Field agreement under continual pressure. As the UMW president, John Mitchell, pointed out to his members:

> *The strength of your union is not the best organised districts. Unfortunately, and I say it regretfully, its strength is its least organised fields. You cannot be permanently safe, you cannot rest in security until West Virginia, the Irwin field, the Connellsville and Meyersdale regions of Pennsylvania, are organised.*[13]

Mitchell's solution was not an organising drive to carry the union into the non-union fields, but a strategy of class collaboration, accepting wage cuts, deteriorating conditions and fragmenting agreements in the Central Competitive Field. This provoked a rank and file revolt that led to the political radicalisation of the union: at the 1908 UMW convention over 400 of the 1,000 delegates were members of the Socialist Party. The union determined to resist further encroachments on the Central Competitive Field agreement and also to make a determined effort to organise the non-union fields.

The attempt to break into the non-union fields produced bloody conflicts in both Colorado and West Virginia. In both states the UMW met with the most fierce resistance. Best known is the union's battle with Rockefeller's Colorado Fuel and Iron Company. On 20 April 1914 company guards and state militia attacked a union tent colony at Ludlow, killing three strikers and 13 women and children. One of the dead miners was the union organiser, Louis Tikas, who was captured by the militia, beaten and summarily executed. By the time the union admitted defeat, nearly 70 people had been killed in this conflict.[14]

Equally bloody was the conflict in West Virginia. Here the UMW had already achieved a foothold in Kanawha County but in April 1912 this came under attack when the mine companies refused to renew agreements. After a two month strike most gave in, but in Paint Creek and Cabin Creek where nearly 100 pits employed 7,500 miners the employers continued to resist. Here the mine companies employed the Baldwin-Felts agency to break the strike and precipitated a small scale war.[15] According to David Corbin in his classic study of the West Virginia miners, *Life, Work and Rebellion in the Coal Fields*:

> *Armed and organised, the striking miners unleashed their rage upon the Baldwin-Felts guards. They hid in the hills and sniped at individual guards, and squads of miners attacked companies of Baldwin-Felts men. In one instance, miners surrounded a camp of guards during the night, cleared away the underbrush, and silently waited till dawn. When the guards awoke and began preparing breakfast, the miners opened fire, killing 13 to 15 of them... The miners blew up the tipples of operating mines and the trains carrying coal that had been mined by scabs. They met trains that were bringing strikebreakers to the strike zone and forced the potential scabs to evacuate—an action that often pitted black strikers against black strikebreakers and immigrant strikers against immigrant strikebreakers. The solidarity of black and white, Protestant and Catholic, immigrant and native miners was unbreakable.*

Hatred of the company guards and private detectives was ferocious. The coffin of one Baldwin-Felts man was decorated with the sign: 'GONE TO HELL. MORE TO GO. DAMNED THUGS'. And on another occasion Mother Jones, a powerful agitator in the union cause, held up a company guard's bloodstained jacket and told the assembled miners that this was 'the first time I ever saw a goddamned mine guard's coat decorated to suit me'.[16]

Despite blanket court injunctions that made union activity illegal, the murderous activities of the Baldwin-Felts agents, the proclamation of martial law, intervention by the National Guard, mass arrests, the suppression of the socialist press and an attempted sell out by UMW officials, the miners emerged victorious. It was this tremendous struggle against all the odds that inspired a Wobbly, Ralph Chaplin, to write the union song 'Solidarity Forever'. As he wrote at the time, 'Solidarity is something more than a word in Kanawha County; it is a tremendous and spontaneous force—a force born in the hot heart of the class struggle.'[17]

But while the union succeeded in consolidating its position in Kanawha County with 16,000 members, southern West Virginia—the counties of Mingo, Logan and McDowell—remained non-union, controlled by company guards, Baldwin-Felts agents and sheriff Don Chafin.

Clearly West Virginia was of crucial importance to the UMW. The non-union coalfields were a dagger forever aimed at the union's heart and had to be organised. What this involved, however, was not a confrontation with backwoods mine companies, petty local tyrants who had never heard of industrial relations, but with corporate interests at the heart of American capitalism. Over 90 percent of the land in Mingo and Logan Counties was owned by outside interests. The powerful Mellon family owned mines in the area, but the dominant interest was the fiercely anti-union corporation, US Steel, that owned over 32,000 acres in Mingo and Logan and another 50,000 acres in McDowell. British companies also had extensive holdings. The fact was that southern West Virginia was not owned and controlled by local capitalists but by capitalists resident in New York, Philadelphia, Boston, Baltimore and London. The decision to wage murderous war on the union was taken by these men.

Post-war struggles

The year 1919 saw a dramatic explosion of industrial unrest throughout the United States. Over 4 million workers were involved in 3,630 strikes. In February there was a general strike in Seattle. Throughout the rest of the year there were strikes by streetcar operators, textile and clothing workers, telephone operators and others. Then in September the Boston police went on strike. The decisive struggles, however, were the great steel strike that began in September and the great miners' strike that began in November. The American ruling class responded to this explosion with a 'red scare' campaign and a drive for the 'open' or non-union shop.

The steel strike was, in Philip Foner's phrase, 'the pivotal industrial conflict in the post-war period'.[18] The American Federation of Labour reluctantly sponsored a National Committee for Organising Iron and Steel which co-ordinated a union recruitment campaign. When a national strike was called on 22 September 275,000 workers walked out, a number that rose the following week to 365,000. The employers, dominated by US Steel stood firm, refused to recognise the unions and resolved to starve and intimidate the strikers back to work. The strike began to crumble. By mid-December the number of workers still out had fallen to 100,000 and the strike was finally called off on 8 January 1920. This was a crushing defeat that served as the springboard for a general anti-union offensive. Between 1920 and 1923 union membership in the United States was to fall by 1.5 million.[19]

Discontent was also building up among the miners with a rash of unofficial strikes in the summer of 1919 and demands for a general strike to secure the release of Tom Mooney[20], a revolutionary socialist framed for a bombing in San Francisco in 1916. This unrest came to a head at the UMW convention in September when delegates voted to demand a six hour day, five day week (at that time miners worked an eight hour day and a six day week, so this would have required an 18 hour reduction) and a 60 percent wage increase. Failure to concede would result in a national strike on 1 November. Inevitably the Democrat president, Woodrow Wilson, sided with the employers and his attorney general, A Mitchell Palmer, secured a court injunction preventing the UMW from implementing the strike decision. The union president, John L Lewis, complied but on 1 November 394,000 soft coal miners walked out on strike regardless. On 8 November the court ordered the union to secure a return to work. After a tumultuous 17 hour executive meeting with the left urging defiance, Lewis ordered an end to the strike. The strike continued and it was not until the end of December that a general return to work had taken place. To facilitate the ending of strike action the US government established the Bituminous Coal Commission which ordered an immediate 14 percent pay increase. When the commission made its final award in March 1920 the average pay rise was 27 percent, but nothing was conceded on hours. This was certainly a partial victory but it failed to exploit to the full the opportunities offered by the militancy of the times. Moreover, continued unrest and widespread unofficial strikes throughout the summer of 1920 secured a further increase in August 1920 that put miners in the organised coalfields on $7.50 a day.[21]

What of the threat of the non-union fields? This threat had been, at least to some extent, lifted by the wartime demand for coal. It now returned with a vengeance. In Alabama the mine owners refused to implement the commission awards and instead imposed wage cuts. Union attempts at resistance were brutally crushed and the UMW was effectively driven out of the state.[22] What of West Virginia?

Bloody Mingo

West Virginia UMW District 17, under the leadership of Frank Keeney and Fred Mooney, both socialists, had successfully consolidated its hold in the northern and western districts. By the end of 1918 they claimed a union membership of 22,000 out of a mine workforce of 100,000, uniting black and white, native and immigrant, in the face of the most brutal repression. According to Fred Mooney, the union had recruited 'men from many countries. Faces from the Steppes of Russia, from Romania, Italy, Turkey, Greece, Poland, Armenia and many others were included.' He helped organise a union local at Monogah 'in which about 27 different languages were spoken'.[23] Racial barriers between black and white workers were broken down by the severity of their common exploitation and oppression. Although racism still infected the consciousness of some white miners, it was overlaid by the need for and achievement of working class unity. Black miners were elected onto District 17's executive, appointed as organisers and served as officers of union locals (one local had a black president, vice-president and secretary). They were in the forefront of the fight against the mine owners.[24]

Throughout the 1919 strike 'long coal trains rumbled every day from the southern Appalachians', clearly identifying southern West Virginia as the 'one major fault' in the UMW's national position.[25] Rank and file miners throughout the country demanded that the hold of the mine owners and their company guards be broken and the region organised. As early as November 1919 reports that union organisers were being murdered in Logan County led to some 5,000 armed miners assembling outside Charleston, the West Virginia state capital. They intended to liberate Logan, drive out the company guards and establish union control. District 17's president, Frank Keeney, persuaded them to disperse. Nevertheless, the UMW was determined to establish itself throughout the state.

Early in 1920 the UMW began organising in Mingo County, using the independent town of Matewan, with its union mayor and chief of police, as a centre of operations. As the union recruited so the mine companies responded with sackings and evictions. What transformed the situation, however, was the unsuccessful attempt by Baldwin-Felts agents to take over Matewan. First Sid Hatfield was offered bribes to allow the agency to establish a guard post equipped with machine guns in the town and then on 19 May the attempt was made to kill him. Hatfield's devastating victory ended the climate of fear maintained by the Baldwin-Felts agents and thousands of miners flooded into the union. By the end of June over 90 percent of the county's miners were enrolled in 34 locals and the union's state wide membership had risen to over 50,000. On 1 July the UMW called its members in Mingo County out on strike.

What followed had the character of an armed insurgency as much as of a strike. Throughout the county armed miners fought it out with company guards and state police, enforcing the closure of the mines. At Mohawk, for example, union delegations were sent into the town on three occasions to persuade the company to remove imported strikebreakers and close the mine. They were unsuccessful. On the fourth occasion hundreds of miners opened fire on the town from the surrounding hills until the company complied. According to Corbin, by early September:

> *the striking Mingo County miners had gained control of most of the county. The state police and company guards did not try to reopen the closed mines. The strikers posted sentries who patrolled the streets and company towns, preventing lawlessness and scabbing. Telephone repairmen were forced to ask the strikers' permission to fix telephone lines that had been shot down during one of the gun battles.*[26]

Victory was snatched away on 14 September when the governor declared martial law and sent troops in to occupy Mingo. The mine owners reopened the mines and imported strikebreakers, while the striking miners suffered a hard winter living in their tent colonies. A guerilla campaign continued throughout the winter months in which a number of soldiers were killed, but the union had lost the initiative and faced defeat by attrition. Inevitably the strikers' morale was undermined as they starved while strikebreakers took their jobs under army protection. Keeney was determined that this should not happen and threatened to extend the strike throughout the whole West Virginia coalfield if the troops were not withdrawn. On 15 February the Governor gave in and the troops were pulled out. The miners now attempted to regain the initiative.

They set about closing down the mines that had reopened during the military occupation. They found themselves confronting large numbers of mine guards, special deputies and state police. A large scale confrontation took place at Merrimac in May. Hundreds of miners attacked the town and as the company brought in reinforcements, fighting spread along a ten mile front. The battle lasted three days and left at least 20 men dead. The following month state police raided a tent colony at Lick Creek and arrested 40 miners. Alex Breedlove, a black miner who had been one of the first men in Mingo to join the union, was singled out and summarily executed. News of this killing outraged union opinion. Clearly the UMW faced an uphill struggle.

Meanwhile pressure was building up for decisive action to support the Mingo miners. Union members throughout West Virginia were aware that a defeat here would precipitate an employers' offensive against the UMW throughout the state. One incident brought this pressure to a head. Sid Hatfield, still a key figure in the union campaign in Mingo, had been charged with organising the attack on Mohawk the previous year and was due to appear in court in the town of Welch in McDowell County. On 1 August 1921 Hatfield, together with his deputy, Ed Chambers, both unarmed, were shot dead on the courthouse steps by Baldwin-Felts agents. Hatfield was shot 15 times when C E Lively walked over, in front of a crowd of onlookers, to finish him off with a bullet in the head. None of those responsible were ever brought to trial. When Hatfield was buried in Matewan 2,000 mourners followed his coffin.

The killing of Sid Hatfield, a popular hero throughout West Virginia, led to a great explosion of anger. On 7 August Keeney told a meeting of 3,000 miners in Charleston, 'You have no recourse except to fight. The only way you can get your rights is with a high-powered rifle, and the man who does not have this equipment is not a good union man.'[27] Meetings were held throughout the organised areas and the miners were urged to assemble in arms at Lens Creek, ten miles south of Charleston on 20 August. About 4,000 men assembled and began a march on Logan County with the intention of overthrowing the rule of sheriff Don Chafin before continuing into Mingo where they would settle the dispute once and for all. Once the march got under way, numbers increased to over 15,000 men, not just miners but other workers as well, coming to strike a blow against the mine companies. According to one account:

> *The strikers constituted a fully-fledged proletarian army, complete with a uniform consisting of overalls with a red bandanna, with red flags tied to their guns, a medical corps, and a variety of arms including one machine gun. Bill Blizzard, a union official, was 'General' of the army.*[28]

The marchers, who included some 2,000 ex-soldiers, were formed into disciplined units, many of them commanded by former officers from a variety of armies. They effectively took control of the area from south of Charleston up to the mountain range surrounding Logan and Mingo Counties.

Meanwhile in Logan County sheriff Don Chafin, the local Democratic Party boss who ran the county on behalf of the mine owners, prepared to resist the invasion. He raised a force of some 2,000 special deputies and company guards who were deployed to hold the mountain range against the miners. Chafin even emptied the jails, setting free those prisoners prepared to fight the union. At least one prisoner, a bricklayer named Comiskey, arrested carrying an IWW card, was shot dead on the spot when he refused to take part.[29]

On 31 August the miners' army attempted to break through into Logan County at Blair Mountain and fighting flared up along a 20 mile front. Chafin hired private aircraft to drop bombs on the miners' camps. Slowly the miners pressed forward in a series of outflanking attacks until they had captured half the mountain ridge. It was only a matter of hours before Chafin's army disintegrated. On 3 September the day was saved by the arrival of over 2,000 US troops sent in by President Harding. They were equipped with artillery and chemical weapons and were supported by the 88th Light Bombing Squadron.[30] They found Chafin and his lieutenants blind drunk. Coincidentally, Harding's secretary of the Treasury, Andrew Mellon, one of the richest men in America, was himself a substantial mine owner in Mingo and Logan Counties.

The union army retreated and dispersed. The attempt to organise southern West Virginia had failed. How many men were killed in the march on Logan and the battle for Blair Mountain is not known. The official estimate was four, but both sides deliberately concealed their casualties and buried their dead in secret. The union's defeat was now followed by a legal offensive. Between September and October 1921 grand juries in Logan County brought in 1,217 indictments for complicity in the insurrection including 325 charges of murder and 24 indictments for treason. Hundreds of miners including Keeney, Mooney and Blizzard were thrown into jail. The trials were held in the courthouse where John Brown had been convicted in 1859. Blizzard was singled out as an example but after a trial lasting over a month he was acquitted in May 1922. The great majority of charges were later dismissed but two miners, a baptist minister, the Reverend J E Wilbur, and his son, were convicted of murder for shooting a special deputy. The last case was not heard until 1924. Writing 50 years later, Art Shields, a socialist journalist who had reported the march on Logan County, summed up 'the biggest armed struggle in US labour history':

> *It was a grass-roots movement, to use an old phrase. It was a movement of men united by strong class feelings. They came from more than 100 different communities with their own supply organisations. The march demonstrated some of the creative qualities of a militant working class that will in time take power. And it left behind a feeling of pride that persists after 50 years.*[31]

The harsh reality of the situation in southern West Virginia was that the employers' determination to resist union organisation was so great they were prepared to mobilise on a scale the miners could not hope to defeat. The intervention of the army in September 1921 made clear that the mine owners' uncompromising stand against the UMW had the full backing of the capitalist state. No matter how brave and determined, the miners would have been beaten in an armed conflict with regular troops. This does not mean that defeat was inevitable. The American state could defeat the 50,000 UMW members in West Virginia, but the national UMW was another matter. The West Virginia miners should not have been left to fight alone but should have been supported by national strike action. This was not an empty pipedream.

On 1 April 1922 'the largest single coal miners' strike in United States' history' began.[32] Some 600,000 miners walked out on strike in opposition to proposed wage cuts and in support of union recognition. Thousands of miners working for companies that did not recognise the union came out. This became the central issue of the dispute because of recognition that the union's long term survival depended on organising the non-union fields. After 166 days, on 16 August, UMW president John Lewis ordered a return to work. The $7.50 a day had been safeguarded but the question of union recognition was conceded. Those thousands of miners who had walked out of non-union mines were left to fight alone and to secure whatever terms they could. This was a disaster. Lewis's betrayal of the 1922 strike was to condemn the UMW to fight a losing war of attrition throughout the 1920s as the unorganised fields succeeded in undermining the organised. By 1928 UMW membership nationally had fallen to 80,000 with Illinois the only area where it had any real strength. Lewis fought off all rank and file challenges to his leadership by a strategy of red baiting, corruption, ballot rigging and gangsterism.[33]

For the miners of West Virginia the 1922 strike was too late. The organising campaign in the southern counties had been defeated and the mine owners followed up their victory by driving the union out of the rest of the state. By 1925 union membership was down to 10,000 of whom over 7,000 were unemployed. The unity between black and white miners was in serious danger as the Ku Klux Klan made headway within the union, a consequence of defeat.[34] The UMW, both locally and nationally, was not to recover from these defeats until the great explosion of labour unrest in the 1930s.[35]

Conclusion

John Sayles's film *Matewan* is a marvellous celebration of working class solidarity and courage in the face of the most brutal employers. It focuses on the rank and file experience of the 1920 strike with the intention of inspiring similar solidarity and courage among the working class today. This is to be wholeheartedly welcomed.

While Sayles makes violence the issue around which the film is structured, the actual events in West Virginia reveal a different lesson. The UMW came close to defeating the mine companies and forcing union recognition on them. This was despite the murderous activities of the company guards and private detectives. What turned the tide was the intervention of the federal government and the arrival of troops and bomber aircraft to crush the miners' army at Blair Mountain. Victory was still possible. National action by the UMW and solidarity action from other unions could still have won the day. Instead the struggle remained localised and despite all their courage, sacrifice and endurance, the miners went down to defeat in West Virginia.

Notes

1 H B Lee, *Bloodletting in Appalachia* (Morganstown, West Virginia, 1969), pp55-56.
2 Ibid, p57.
3 R L Lewis, *Black Coal Miners in America* (Lexington, Kentucky, 1987), p164.
4 J Hillier, *The New Hollywood* (London, 1993), p47.
5 Sayles has published one other novel, *Pride of the Bimbos,* about a drag softball team and a collection of short stories, *The Anarchists Convention.*
6 J Sayles, *Thinking In Pictures* (Boston, 1987), pp9-11. This is Sayles's own account of the making of *Matewan* and includes the screenplay.
7 Ibid, pp16-17.
8 D P Jordan, 'The Mingo War: Labor Violence in the Southern West Virginia Coal Fields 1919-1922', in G M Fink and M E Reed (eds), *Essays in Southern Labor History* (Westport, Connecticut, 1976), p119.
9 S Brier, 'A History Film Without Much History', *Radical History Review* 41 (1988), pp123, 125. Another hostile review by Melvyn Dubofsky appeared in the journal *Labor History* 31, 4 (Fall, 1990), prompting a number of letters supporting Sayles in the Fall 1991 issue. For sympathetic reviews of the film see in particular P S Foner, '*Matewan*: The story behind the movie', *Political Affairs* (January 1988) and R Lewis, '*Matewan*', *Journal of American History* 75 (1988).
10 J Sayles, op cit, p34.
11 J P Johnson, *The Politics of Soft Coal* (Urbana, Illinois, 1979), p26.
12 D Montgomery, *The Fall of the House of Labour* (New York, 1987), p342.
13 A F Hinrichs, *The United Mine Workers of America and the Non-Union Coal Fields* (New York, 1923), p119.
14 See Z Papanikolas, *Buried Unsung: Louis Takas and the Ludlow Massacre* (Lincoln, Nebraska, 1991).
15 The Baldwin-Felts agency had been established in the 1890s and was first used to strikebreak in the West Virginia coalfield in 1902. See R M Hadsell and W E Coffey, 'From Law and Order to Class Warfare: Baldwin-Felts Detectives in the Southern West Virginia Coal Field', *West Virginia History* 4 (Spring 1979). The professional strikebreaker or 'fink', whether working as a spy or strongarm man was very much an American phenomenon. Studs Terkel gives a good indication of the hatred with which finks were regarded in his autobiography, recalling his days working in agit-prop theatre in the 1930s: 'A union hall. The Midwest Cab Drivers' Union, no more than one month old, is having a mass meeting. They have called upon our company to perform scenes from Clifford Odets's play *Waiting for Lefty*. It is highly appropriate, dealing as it does with a cab drivers' strike. Its locale is poetically enough a union hall. Something happens this evening wholly unplanned. In the play, a striker exposes his brother as a fink. The actor, portraying the fink, runs off the stage, through the aisle, and out. On this occasion, he doesn't quite make it. The realism is too much for the striking cabbies in the audience. Several reach out and clobber the unfortunate actor. I, playing the role of his brother, holler, "Don't slug him, don't slug him, he's only an actor!" ' From Studs Terkel, *Talking To Myself* (London, 1986), p120.
16 D Corbin, *Life, Work and Rebellion in the Coal Fields* (Urbana, Illinois, 1981), pp90-91. This is a volume in the University of Illinois Press's excellent 'The

Working Class in American History' series which is unfortunately not distributed in this country.

17 Ibid, p91.

18 P S Foner, *History of the Labor Movement in the United States: Postwar Struggles 1918-1920* (New York, 1988), p148.

19 For the 1919 steel workers' strike see D Brody, *Labor in Crisis: The Steel Strike of 1919* (New York, 1965).

20 Mooney had been involved in an unsuccessful attempt to organise San Francisco's car men. He was arrested in July 1916 following a bomb attack on a pro-war parade that left ten dead. Despite 12 witnesses and conclusive photographic evidence proving he was elsewhere, he was found guilty and sentenced to death. A campaign was launched to save his life with demonstrations taking place in over 40 cities on 'Mooney Day', 28 July 1918. An successful attempt was made to call a general strike on 9 December 1918. The protest did save his life with the sentence being commuted to life imprisonment. The campaign to secure his release continued throughout the 1920s and 1930s. He was finally released in January 1939, returning to San Francisco at the head of a celebratory parade and going on to address a rally of 25,000 people. See R H Frost, *The Mooney Case* (Stanford, California, 1968).

21 For a discussion of Lewis's role see P S Foner, op cit, pp146-148.

22 In Alabama nearly 80 percent of the UMW's members were black. For the 1920 strike see R Straw, 'The United Mine Workers of America and the 1920 Coal Strike in Alabama', *Alabama Review* 18 (April 1975) and G Feldman, 'Labour Repression in the American South: Corporations, State and Race in Alabama's Coal Fields 1917-1921', *Historical Journal* 37, 2 (June 1994).

23 F Mooney, *Struggle in the Coal Fields* (Morganstown, West Virginia, 1967), p60.

24 D Corbin, op cit, pp76-79; R L Lewis, op cit, pp156-164. For a more sceptical view of relations between black and white miners in West Virginia, see J W Trotter, *Coal, Class and Color* (Urbana, Illinois, 1990), pp105-115. For the UMW and black miners generally, see H Gutman's essay, 'The Negro and the United Mine Workers of America', which is collected in his *Work, Culture and Society in Industrializing America* (Oxford, 1977). This essay has been the subject of a heated academic exchange: H Hill, 'Myth-Making as Labor History: Herbert Gutman and the United Mine Workers of America' *Politics, Culture and Society* 2, 2 (Winter 1988), and S Brier, 'In Defence of Gutman: The Union's Case', *Politics, Culture and Society* 2, 3 (Spring, 1989).See also Rick Halpern,'Organized Labour, Black Workers and the 20th Century South: the emerging revision', *Social History* 19,3 (Octorber 1994). For an excellent overview of the question of black and white working class unity, see L Sustar, 'The Roots of Multi-racial Labour Unity in the United States', *International Socialism* 63 (Summer 1994).

25 L Savage, *Thunder in the Mountains* (Pittsburgh, 1990), p14.

26 D Corbin, op cit, p204.

27 Ibid, p217.

28 H N Wheeler, 'Mountaineer Mine Wars: An Analysis of the West Virginia Mine Wars of 1912-13 and 1920-21', *Business History Review* 50 (Spring 1976), p80.

29 H B Lee, op cit, pp99-100; L Savage, op cit, pp140-141.

30 M Maurer and C Senning, 'Billy Mitchell, The Air Service and The Mingo War', *West Virginia History* 38 (1968), p343. Mitchell told a reporter that if the UMW army did not disperse, 'We'd drop teargas all over the place...then we'd open up with artillery preparation and everything'.

31 P S Foner, op cit, p227.

32 M Dubofsky and W Van Tine, *John L Lewis* (New York, 1977), p82.

33 John L Lewis is probably the most remarkable opportunist in international, let alone US, labour history. One recent study of the UMW assesses his career up to 1933: 'His years in office to that point had been filled with the almost virtual destruction of the United Mine Workers… It had lost its contracts, its wage scales, its membership. Its once great treasury, the pride of America's unions, was thin and insecure. It had no strength to resist the operators, who could even count on the support of Lewis himself when they needed it. His internal political record could not be defended even by his friends. No man was permitted to defy him. Those who fought him could face almost sure expulsion from the union. Others like Hapgood and Germer and many more could expect beatings that would almost kill them… The charge of vote stealing could be maintained, based upon the shameful evidence of the 1926 campaign… He often supported coal companies against his own men, wiping out an anthracite strike in Pennsylvania in 1931… He was regularly called one of the most reactionary men in American labour, with no program, no vision, no concept of the future', J Finley, *The Corrupt Kingdom* (New York, 1972), pp73-74. This reactionary union boss was to go on to become one of the leaders of the great working class revolt of the 1930s, beginning with a campaign to rebuild the UMW in 1933. He was the architect of the Congress of Industrial Organizations (CIO). No one could better exemplify the ability of the union bureaucrat to face left in order to remain at the head of the movement. Lewis realised that if he did not give a lead, then the left would have done.

34 P S Foner, *Organised Labor and the Black Worker 1619-1973* (New York, 1973), pp169-170.

35 For the great revolt see A Preiss, *Labor's Giant Step* (New York, 1972), and I Bernstein, *Turbulent Years* (Boston, 1971).

The light and the dark

A review of Eric Hobsbawm, ***Age of Extremes, The Short Twentieth Century 1914-1991*** *(London, 1994), £20*

JOHN REES

The opening pages of Eric Hobsbawm's great panorama of the 20th century are devoted to a series of 12 quotations from famous intellectuals, each no more than a sentence or two long, in which they struggle to catch the essence of their century. These views fall into three broad categories—optimists, pessimists and the fashionably agnostic.

For a minority, it is, in spite of everything, a century of scientific or human progress. 'There have been revolutions for the better in this century', as Rita Levi Montalcini, the Italian Nobel prize winner, argues, citing the 'emergence of women after centuries of repression'.

The majority, however, incline to pessimism. In the case of novelist and concentration camp survivor Primo Levi such emotions are only too understandable. But even Isaiah Berlin and Spanish anthropologist Julio Caro Baroja, who both admit having suffered no personal hardship, find their age, respectively, 'the most terrible century in Western history' and a century of 'terrible events which humanity has lived through'. For writer William Golding it is 'the most violent century in human history'.

Fashionable agnosticism is perhaps under-represented by historian Franco Venturi. His remarks are composed of two sentences, the first of which seems to be a resignation note for his whole profession: 'Historians can't answer this question'. But, in the way of academics, his second sentence is a lifetime re-employment contract: 'For me the 20th century is only the ever-renewed effort to understand it.'

It is not the least of Eric Hobsbawm's virtues that he has stood out against this kind of postmodern defeatism. He is still committed to the idea that history can be understood, can be explained, and that there is a difference between the subjective prejudices of the writer and the real events which are being described.

A still greater virtue is that Hobsbawm does not give in to either the facile optimism or the understandable pessimism displayed by the comments he gathers together on the opening pages of the *Age of Extremes*. As the book's title suggests, Hobsbawm sees the contradictory nature of our world: unimaginable wealth piled high beside indescribable poverty, machinery capable of unheard of productivity standing beside unbelievably destructive weapons, the most inhumane and brutal oppression calling forth the most courageous and principled resistance. Perhaps Yehudi Menuhin comes closest to catching this mood when he describes the century as one which has 'destroyed all illusions and ideals' yet also 'raised the greatest hopes ever conceived by humanity'.

The structure of the *Age of Extremes* follows this pattern. It rightly sees the first half of the 20th century as the 'Age of Catastrophe'—the period of the First World War, the rise of Italian fascism, the demise of the Russian Revolution, the slump of the 1930s, the rise of Nazi Germany, the defeat of the Spanish Revolution, and the Second World War. The second part of the book, 'The Golden Age', traces the long post-war boom which accompanied the Cold War and decolonisation. Finally, 'The Landslide' charts the collapse of economic prosperity, the end of Stalinism (or socialism as Hobsbawm mistakenly calls it), the close of the Cold War and the re-emergence of economic crisis and political instability.

All this means that Hobsbawm has the broad measure of a century which threatened, even in its most prosperous years, mass destruction and which called forth, even in its blackest moments, forces which could secure a better world. This alone sets Hobsbawm apart from those theorists who assume that the history of the century, especially that of its closing years, self evidently shows the superiority of liberal democracy and free market capitalism—former US state department official Francis Fukuyama is probably the best known.[1] It also mostly sets Hobsbawm apart from those determinists for whom the growth of the world's population and the progress of technology spell the doom of humanity, although *Age of Extremes* is not entirely above giving way to this kind of millennial gloom on occasions.[2]

Sometimes these strengths carry over into Hobsbawm's account of the turning points of 20th century history. He is generally good, for instance, on Lenin and the Russian Revolution.[3] Hobsbawm stayed in the British Communist Party until it collapsed and so will have heard the

McCarthyite view of the Bolsheviks all too frequently the first time round to be overly impressed now that it is being recycled in the wake of events in Eastern Europe. He is insistent that 'Contrary to the Cold War mythology, which saw Lenin essentially as an organiser of coups, the only real asset he and the Bolsheviks had was the ability to recognise what the masses wanted; to, as it were, lead by knowing how to follow'.[4] More surprisingly, Hobsbawm gives due weight to the central perspective of the October Revolution:

> *Lenin's programme...gamble*[d] *on the conversion of the Russian Revolution into a world, or at least a European, revolution. Who—he said so often enough—could imagine that a victory for socialism 'can come about...except by the complete destruction of the Russian and European bourgeoisie'?*[5]

Hobsbawm is similarly clear sighted about how the 'years of unbroken crisis and catastrophe, German conquest and penal peace, regional breakaways, counter-revolution, civil war, foreign armed intervention, hunger and economic collapse' undermined the revolution. The Bolsheviks, he rightly argues:

> *could have no strategy or perspective beyond choosing, day by day, between decisions needed for immediate survival and the ones which risked immediate disaster. Who could afford to consider the long term consequences for the revolution of decisions which had to be taken now, or else there would be an end to the revolution and no further consequences to consider?*[6]

But once outside the narrow confines of the immediate revolutionary events Hobsbawm's political background begins to show its darker side. It was Stalin who formulated the theory of 'socialism in one country', denying the possibility of Russia relying on the potential of world revolution. Hobsbawm seems to supply retrospective justification for this view. So, although we are told that 'a wave of revolution swept across the globe in the two years after October, and the hopes of the embattled Bolsheviks did not seem unrealistic', the general impression given does not do justice to the depth of the world revolution or to how close it came to hitting its mark. The crucial German revolution is, for instance, described at one point as 'an illusion' since 'the bulk of German revolutionary soldiers, sailors and workers remained...moderate and law abiding'.[7]

Since Hobsbawm underestimates the intensity of the revolutionary upsurge, he is under no special obligation to explain its failure, which had a good deal to do with the Stalinisation of the Communist International. Nor does he have to present the rise of the Stalinist bureaucracy as anything other than the regrettable but unavoidable result of the pressure of events. This then establishes the continuity between the revolutionary era and the whole subsequent history of Stalinism—so that the chapter on world revolution generalises wildly and unconvincingly past the 1920s and on to Mao's China and the 'second great wave of world revolution, from 1944 to 1949', by which he appears to mean the invasion of Eastern Europe by the Russian army.[8]

Indeed, Hobsbawm even goes so far as to write of the post-war world that 'the net effect of 12 years of National Socialism was that large parts of Europe now lay at the mercy of the Bolsheviks'.[9] Yet he knows that virtually the entire leadership of the Bolshevik Party and a great proportion of its rank and file of 1917 had vanished into Stalin's gulag during the 1930s. Certainly there was nothing of it remaining by 1945. Failure to acknowledge the reality and completeness of this counter-revolution necessarily distorts Hobsbawm's view of the century.

The shame of *Age of Extremes* is that the strengths of Hobsbawm's generally Marxist approach are so often cancelled by the legacy of his politics. The actual historical account therefore becomes an infuriating mix of interesting detail and description coupled to a failure to really *explain* the turning points of 20th century history.[10]

Nothing could better illustrate the bind in which Hobsbawm finds himself than his account of the Spanish Revolution of 1936. We are told that 'the Spanish people's reaction to the [Franco] coup was undoubtedly revolutionary' and that, in spite of this, 'the Spanish government and, more to the point, the communists who were increasingly influential in its affairs, insisted that social revolution was not their object, and, indeed, visibly did everything within their power to control and reverse it, to the horror of revolutionary enthusiasts'. He goes on, with commendable honesty, to admit that:

> *The interesting point is that this was not mere opportunism or, as the purists on the ultra Left thought, treason to the revolution. It reflected a deliberate shift from an insurrectionary to a gradualist,...even a parliamentary, way to power.*[11]

This electoralist approach is then praised because it described 'with considerable accuracy the shape of politics in the anti-fascist war of 1939-45' and that 'the logic of anti-fascist war led towards the Left'.

The remarkable fact in all this is that we are never given any account of why, when confronted with such a successful policy, Franco triumphed. Neither are we told how it was that the poor old wrongheaded 'revolutionary purists' (in fact, figures as politically divergent as Trotsky and Independent Labour Party member George Orwell) were able to predict that the Communist Party's policy would lead to the fall of the Republican government and to the destruction of the CP itself.

In reality of course the CP's policy amounted to a policy of counter-revolution. It paralysed and disorganised working class resistance to Franco just when it most needed to be extended and defended. The CP attacked both physically and politically the leaders and organisations of the Spanish Revolution and used the authority they derived from the support given to the Republican forces by the USSR to ensure that the government bent to their will. Hobsbawm's sole gesture towards explaining the defeat of the Republican side is to point to its internal divisions. But the CP was responsible for helping to create these divisions and for resolving them at the expense of workers' control in the factories, the agrarian revolution and the existence of any organisation to the left of the CP. When the revolutionary momentum was halted, the right wing punished the error ruthlessly.[12]

And while the course of the Second World War certainly radicalised working people throughout Europe, it was the CP's new found parliamentarianism which prevented this from resulting in any far reaching social transformation. Crucially, for instance, it brought Italian workers four generations of right wing government and French workers the de Gaulle regime. In both cases the CP's strategy led to their own exclusion from real influence.[13] Certainly the logic of war led to the left, but the logic of the CP's strategy led to defeat.

But Hobsbawm's residual attachment to the disappeared world of Moscow centred 'communism' carries an even greater disabling burden: his explanation of the rise and fall of the long post-war boom, necessarily entailing an account of the collapse of the Eastern bloc, never rises above the level of description. The fundamental role of arms spending in sustaining and then destroying the boom is never analysed because to do so would mean seeing the Eastern bloc as regimes whose military and economic competition with the West defined the nature of the post-war world economy.[14] The way in which arms spending first boosted the world economy and then, since it was unequally born by the major powers, undermined the competitiveness of its biggest contributors and therefore its own effectiveness, is not fully grasped.

Even so, the insight and detail are often impressive—the chapter on 'Third World and Revolution', for instance, is strong on the class make up and aims of the leaders of the Third World revolutions of the 1950s to 1970s. The way in which the popular image of guerrilla struggles has obscured the contribution of working class actions to the process of decolonisation is well described. The fact that the leaders of these revolutions were young and middle class and the fact that they often harked back to an older, pre-1917 tradition of agrarian struggle is usefully recalled. The distance between their political programme—land reform plus modernisation plus national independence—and the original Marxist conception of revolution has been obscured by the Cold War desire to see every threat to American interests as emanating from Moscow. Hobsbawm redresses the balance. But still the significance of all this in the wider history of the Cold War is undermined by the weakness of the theoretical framework which cannot stand the weight of explanation demanded of it.

The same flaw reappears time and again. It is there in the cringe inducing praise for Gorbachev and the snide asides reserved almost exclusively for any political current to the left of the CP. Worst of all, Hobsbawn accepts that political defeat and technological change have undermined the power of the organised working class and so eroded both the possibility of revolution and the voting base of Labour and social democratic parties. This last claim is an extension of his original article, 'The Forward March of Labour Halted', published in the now defunct *Marxism Today*. It is a rather strange conclusion when, for instance, France has had a Socialist Party president, Spain a Socialist Party government and Sweden has had a social democrat government for nearly as long as the Tories have been in power in Britain—and when even here the Labour Party is now 40 points ahead of the Tories in opinion polls.

There are two other faults which, although minor, are worth noting. The first is that Hobsbawm has chosen to inject a personal tone into his narrative which is often irrelevant and nearly always irritating. Is it, for instance, the best way of illustrating the debilitating specialisation which has developed in academia in the 20th century to be told that Hobsbawm himself was at Cambridge at the same time as Crick and Watson were discovering the structure of DNA and that, 'though I even recall meeting Crick socially at the time, most of us were simply not aware that these extraordinary developments were being hatched within a few tens of yards of my college gates, in laboratories we passed regularly and pubs where we drank'?[15] Hobsbawm, like Woody Allen's Leo Zelig, seems to pop up all over the century giving us his particular view of events. But memoir and history, particularly the kind of grand history that Hobsbawm specialises in, are not comfortable bedfellows.

A second, related, point is that the personal judgments which Hobsbawm makes often seem based on no more than the kind of ill tempered snobbiness which readers expect from letter writers to the *Daily Telegraph*. What does it mean for Hobsbawm to tell us that 'no one who has been asked by an intelligent American student whether the phrase "Second World War" meant that there had been a "First World War" is unaware that knowledge of even the basic facts of the century cannot be taken for granted'?[16] Is this the reflex anti-Americanism so common among CP members during the Cold War, or a lament for declining standards in education, or a donnish joke? Take your pick—but any one of them diminishes a book like this.

Similarly, Hobsbawm tells us that for his generation history was 'part of the texture of our lives' (in a way which it is not for younger people) because 'streets and public places were still called after public men and events (the Wilson station in pre-war Prague, the Metro Stalingrad in Paris), when peace treaties were still signed and therefore had to be identified (Treaty of Versailles)...'[17] Now, were Hobsbawm to take a short trip outside his Hampstead home he might come across Hackney's CLR James Library (named after the black nationalist and sometime Trotskyist), the Isle of Dogs' Jack Dash House (after the CP dockers' leader), the huge granite head of Nelson Mandela outside the Royal Festival Hall (and a number of streets and public buildings now bearing his name) or the carved head of black nationalist Marcus Garvey in the entrance hall of the Tottenham Leisure Centre. And a brief glimpse at the daily papers might reveal not only that treaties continue to be signed (for instance, SALT I, SALT II and START) but that they are also sometimes still named after places (the treaties of Rome and Maastricht spring to mind).

This bad humour is more than the product of a liverish disposition or old age. It is the mark of a historian who knows that the century is ending as badly as it began, confronting humanity with the choice described in the *Communist Manifesto*: 'either social revolution or the common ruin of the contending classes'.[18] Such a stark choice is inevitably posed once we raise our eyes from the small events of everyday life and look back over a century which has seen more wars and revolutions, more social crises and catastrophes, than any previous 100 year period. For those Marxists of Hobsbawm's generation the decision for or against socialism was inevitably bound to the question of whether they were for or against Stalinism. Yet to be for Stalin was to be against genuine socialism and democracy in Russia and, eventually, as the Spanish Revolution demonstrated beyond question, everywhere else.

For a long time Hobsbawm's historical work could avoid meeting this fact head on. As he has often said, the tacit agreement between the CP and the CP historians' group was that they could be mostly free of party control so long as they avoided writing about the 20th century. Hobsbawm kept the bargain until the end, loyally elaborating the CP line where current politics were concerned but staying safely in the long 19th century when it came to historical writing. The death of the CP has released him from that bargain, but not from the attitude of mind which went with it. *Age of Extremes* is, consequently, a huge landscape painting of the century, but one painted by an artist who has lost his sense of perspective. And so, despite his initial denial of pessimism, Hobsbawm's world stands in shadow, repeating the dilemma with which it opened:

> *If humanity is to have a recognisable future, it cannot be by prolonging the past or the present. If we try to build the third millennium on that basis, we shall fail. And the price of failure, that is to say, the alternative to a changed society, is darkness.*

These very last sentences are a clarion call for change, but one issued more in the hope than the expectation that it will be answered. Hobsbawm's version of Marxism can see the contradiction at the heart of the century but has long since failed to explain how working people can resolve it.

Notes

1 See his *The End of History and the Last Man* (Penguin, 1993).
2 See, for instance, P Kennedy, *Preparing for the 21st Century* (London, 1993).
3 Hobsbawm seems, in this respect at least, to have recovered his composure after the shock of the collapse of the Eastern European regimes. His initial reaction was to distance himself much more completely from the whole experience of the October revolution. See his 'Waking from History's Great Dream', *Independent on Sunday*, 4 February 1990, where the Russian Revolution is described as 'a freak result' of the age of catastrophe which might have been avoided if the Bolsheviks had heeded Menshevik warnings.
4 E Hobsbawm, *Age of Extremes* (London, 1994), p61.
5 Ibid, p63.
6 Ibid, p64.
7 Ibid, p68.
8 Ibid, p75.
9 Ibid, p175.
10 Perry Anderson has made a similar point in his *Guardian* review: 'Hobsbawm stresses that the purpose of his book is to explain, not to describe events. But at three crucial turning points—the Great Depression, the onset of the post-war boom, and the slide into "stagflation"—he admits that real explanation lies beyond its scope, settling essentially for description.'
11 E Hobsbawm, op cit, p162.
12 It was only the Bolsheviks' insistence on deepening the revolution in the face of the attempted military coup headed by Kornilov in 1917 which prevented, as Trotsky put it, fascism being a Russian rather than an Italian word.
13 See, for instance, the masterly *Politics of War* by Gabriel Kolko (second ed, New York, 1990).
14 For an account of the arms economy see A Callinicos, J Rees, C Harman and M Haynes, *Marxism and the New Imperialism* (London, 1994); C Harman, *Explaining the Crisis* (London, 1987); M Kidron, *Western Capitalism Since the War* (London, 1968).
15 E Hobsbawm, op cit, p527.
16 Ibid, p3.
17 Ibid, p4.

18 This non-deterministic approach was central to Marx, quite contrary to Hobsbawm's claim that, for Marx, 'the class struggle between the bourgeoisie and the proletariat…could only have one outcome.' As footnote 17 above, p57.

How to make the Tories disappear

A review of David Butler, Andrew Adonis and Tony Travers, ***Failure in British Government—the Politics of the Poll Tax*** *(Oxford University Press) £7.99, and Paul Whiteley, Patrick Seyd and Jeremy Richardson,* ***True Blues—the Politics of Conservative Party Membership*** *(Oxford University Press) £12.95*

JUDY COX

John Major now presides over the most unpopular government since records began, but that's not the only problem facing the Conservative Party—the party itself is in long term decline with membership shrinking and commitment weakening.

In response to the current malaise many Tories hark back to the 'golden days' of Thatcherism, but new research detailed in the book *True Blues* shows that during Thatcher's premiership the decline of the Tory Party actually accelerated. Another new book shows how the Tories' attempts to introduce the poll tax undermined their own support. The authors of *Failure in British Politics* set out to explain how the government came to introduce a policy as suicidal as the poll tax. The tax has been seen as a simple aberration or a product of Thatcher's increasingly megalomaniac personality. Accident and egomania may have played a role, but the introduction and forced abandonment of the poll tax really illustrate more fundamental conflicts within the Conservative Party.

The Tory Party is divided because it serves the interests of the ruling class, but its membership also includes many members of the middle class. During deep economic crises these two sections of the party can have different interests. So, while it is the poor who have undoubtedly suffered the most under the Tories, the government's increasingly desperate measures have pulled wider and wider layers of society into opposition and even, at times, active resistance. The poll tax is only one especially dramatic example of this process. The whole episode of the poll tax also shows that, while the Conservative Party is ripped apart by internal divisions, it is not enough to simply wait for it to commit collective suicide. This is what ex Labour leader Neil Kinnock discovered when he lost the 1992 general election.

True Blues is really aimed at social scientists, but among the statistics and equations are some revealing facts. Amazing as it may seem today, the Conservative Party is one of the most successful parliamentary parties of all time. The Tories have held office for all but 28 years this century. They have been in office for 73 percent of the time since 1950. Despite this the Conservative Party is now in serious decline. The average age of Conservative Party members is 62, almost half are over 66. This means that around 40 percent of the party will die over the next ten years!

Party members are not only old, they are inactive. Only 18 percent even display election posters (many admitted to being afraid of social ostracism if they did). The two most common reasons for people joining the Tories is either 'to oppose the Labour Party or trade unions' or for 'social reasons'.[1] These take precedence over any loyalty to the Conservative Party or commitment to its principles. In their study, Whiteley, Seyd and Richardson estimate that since 1960 the membership of the party has been declining by 64,000 a year and will be less than 100,000 by the end of the century. Personal donations to the party fell from £14 million in 1992 to only £3 million in 1993, the worst fall since Conservative Party records began.

True Blues confirms that, while the Conservative Party represents the interests of big capitalists and the ruling class as a whole, its members come from the petty bourgeoisie. This is clearly seen in the area of education. Private education has always been important to Conservative politics, and many MPs are educated at fee paying schools. But the majority of party members left school at 16, and only about one quarter went to private schools. Most members are neither rich nor poor. Less than 10 percent of the party is made up of working class members (these are mostly farm workers) and a further 6 percent are foremen and technicians. At the other end of the scale, only 8 percent have household incomes of more than £50,000.

The vast majority of Conservative Party members work in the private sector of the economy. An overwhelming 91 percent own their own homes. Only 4 percent took advantage of the Tories' right to buy policies —most had owned their own homes for years. It is a similar picture with the government's privatisation of public industries; many Tory Party members bought shares but 70 percent owned stocks and shares before the privatisation share issues. Members of the Conservative Party are a lot older and more middle class than the people who vote for it.

Significantly, about 40 percent of the members believe that they have risen up the class structure from working class families. They see themselves as upwardly mobile and are terrified of being thrust back into the poverty from which they have escaped.

The membership of the Conservative Party underwent a significant change during the Thatcher years. From the late 1970s onwards the new members who joined were much less active and committed to the party. Thatcher is remembered as the champion of grass roots party members but, in reality, the most active Tories were usually 'wets' who disliked her ruthless attacks on the welfare state. Successive Thatcher governments set out to weaken the power of local councils, many of which were Labour controlled during the 1980s. Ironically, many party members say that the chance to get involved in local government was an important incentive for joining the Conservatives. By launching a campaign against local councils, the Thatcher government undermined recruitment to their own party.

The existence of local government gives Tory party members the feeling that they can influence local affairs, but the number who actually get involved in institutions of local authority (local councillors, special constables etc) is actually quite limited. The party, however, is still so large that if only 1 percent are magistrates this amounts to a total of 7,500 people, giving the Tories considerable influence. The study does not deal with the massive growth of quangos which are overwhelmingly staffed by Tories. However, from the figures available it appears that grass roots Tories have not been involved in the quango gravy train, the real beneficiaries being from the upper echelons of the the party.

Thatcher's flagship

With hindsight it seems almost incomprehensible that the Thatcher government should have attempted to introduce such a blatantly regressive tax as the poll tax. No government had seriously considered the poll tax as an option since 1381 when a similar tax sparked the peasants' revolt. In the 1980s the Tories had two great incentives to abolish the rates system of raising funds for local government. The first was an economically motivated drive to slash public spending. The other was an ideologically driven attempt to reorganise local government.

The rating systems had long been hated by the Tories because tax levels were linked to ability to pay. In fact, they were not very keen on local government as a whole. Nicholas Ridley, who was to take a turn as minister in charge of the poll tax, expressed a commonly felt hostility to all local government. He wrote in a controversial Centre for Policy

Studies pamphlet that 'inefficiency is not, I regret to say, confined to councils run by the Terrible Trots'.[2]

This dislike was fed by the rise of municipal socialism in the early 1980s, when Labour left wingers took over many big metropolitan councils. 'Red Ken' Livingstone, leader of the Greater London Council, became a hate figure in the Tory tabloids. In Liverpool the *Militant* dominated council forced the government to reach a financial compromise which caused shock waves among the establishment. The headline of The *Economist* was 'Liverpool millions, Jenkin nil' (Jenkin was minister for the environment). The government and the Tory tabloids whipped up a hysterical campaign against the Labour run councils.

This was typical of the Thatcher government's method of dealing with those who resisted its policies. First the government would launch a campaign to demonise any potential enemy. The National Union of Mineworkers became the 'enemy within' and the councils were all run by the 'loony left'. Then the isolated opponents could be picked off one at a time.

To reinforce the campaign against the rates system senior Tories constantly talked about 'little old ladies', often widows, who were paying the same rates as households full of wage earners. The language used by different ministers was curiously similar. Thatcher's recollection of the time is typical: 'I witnessed a chorus of complaints from people living alone—widows for example—who consumed far less of local authority services than the large family next door with several working sons, but who were expected to pay the same rates bills'.[3] Never before or since had little old ladies provoked such a storm of emotion among Tory politicians. In fact, there was no evidence that any ministers were inundated with such complaints.

This campaign developed a momentum of its own. The Tory party leadership is famous for the contempt in which it holds ordinary party members. The party members have no influence over policy or party organisation. A majority of party members themselves do not think that the leadership listens to their views.[4] This attitude is summed up by ex-leader Arthur Balfour's famous comment that he would rather take the advice of his valet than consult the Tory Party conference.[5] However, plans to introduce the poll tax went forward in great leaps at every annual conference. This was not the result of consultation with the conference delegates. Rather it was because the conference, which acts as a crucial stage on which ministers with ambitions have to perform well, demands that any Tory with leadership pretensions must turn up with something designed to win the adulation of the faithful. The leadership had created the monster of the 'loony left' councils, so they had to be seen to be able to slay it. The ambitions of various Tory ministers helped increase the momentum for the introduction of the poll tax.

The whole cabinet was convinced that getting rid of the rates, at whatever the cost, would be popular. Their great confidence was based on very flimsy evidence. For Thatcher, it was a simple matter of gut feeling:

> *Deep in their instincts people find what I am saying and doing right and I know it is because it is the way I was brought up in a small town. We knew everyone, we knew what people thought. I sort of regard myself as a very normal, ordinary person with all the right instinctive antennae.*[6]

Thatcher's antennae proved to be inaccurate not simply because of her own arrogance but because the Tory leaders' contempt for democracy meant they could not gauge the mood of their own party, never mind that the wider electorate. So Thatcher called the poll tax the 'flagship of the Thatcher fleet', and Nicholas Ridley, minister for the environment, bragged that the tax was fair because a duke would pay the same as a dustman.

The cabinet insisted on believing that the poll tax would be lower than the rates despite evidence as early as 1987 that it would be much higher than the rates in many areas, not just in Labour run inner cities. The impression given by the memoirs quoted in *Failure in British Politics* is that ministers really believed that if they repeated the lie often enough it would become true. They were so confident that they abandoned plans to introduce the tax gradually and to cushion its impact.

The Tories' strategy of lying about the levels of the tax simply increased taxpayers' sense of shock when the real bills arrived. In Scotland the bills were the signal for mass protests which spread south when the tax hit England. Hundreds of thousands faced the courts because they refused to pay the tax. By spring 1990 the revolt was massive. Every time councils around the country met to set a rate they were greeted by mass demonstrations, some turning into riots when the police intervened.

In March 1990 the Tories lost the Mid-Staffordshire by-election—a 'safe seat' lost by what was then a record 22 percent swing to Labour. The campaign culminated in the All-Britain Anti-Poll Tax Federation marches in London and Edinburgh. A major riot erupted when police attacked the London march. Scaffolding and buildings were set alight, and the rioting spread across Soho, Charing Cross and Covent Garden, and became an international news story.

The government was shocked by the fact that everyone blamed them, not the councils, for the huge tax bills and the mass protests. Even Tories blamed the government—the whole of the ruling Conservative group on

West Oxfordshire Council resigned in protest against the tax. The Tories hoped that Labour would be blamed for the violence at the Trafalgar Square demonstration. In fact Labour's support went up. To her horror, Thatcher realised that she had succeeded making 'law abiding, decent people' side with 'the mob'.[7]

The riots had a massive impact. After them only a few diehard ministers, like Michael Portillo, continued to support the tax. Thatcher's days were numbered. But the Tory party did not only lose their prime minister—£1.5 billion was lost administering the tax, in addition to the £20 billion costs and a further £6 billion on local tax bills.

It is incredible that during the long process of drafting and bringing in the poll tax so few voices were raised against it. The poll tax debacle shows the undemocratic nature of a parliamentary system supposedly able to prevent such disasters from happening. Once the tax was approved by the Tory leadership, anyone who raised doubts about it would be considered a 'wet' and their careers suffered accordingly. Few MPs were prepared to sacrifice their careers. This was as true of the civil servants involved as it was of ministers like Kenneth Baker and William Waldegrave who were initially in charge of the tax. The House of Lords was far too spineless to vote against the poll tax, especially because, in a cynical move, lots of old Tories were wheeled out to ensure the bill introducing the tax was passed (it was one of the largest turnouts ever for a vote in the Lords).

The official parliamentary opposition, the Labour Party, was not much better. *Failure in British Government* exposes Labour's failure to oppose the poll tax, either in parliament or outside it. The Labour leader, Neil Kinnock, seemed as intent on attacking *Militant* supporters as he was on attacking the government, and refused to support the non-payment campaigns:

> *Tony Benn, exasperated by his inability to get Kinnock to support the ill-fated Trafalgar Square rally in the spring of 1990, told his diary: 'The Labour Party is more frightened of the anti poll tax campaign than of the poll tax itself.' He was not far off the mark.*[8]

Thousands of people switched to supporting Labour because they hated the tax, even though the Labour leaders did nothing to oppose it. Labour's support was at its peak after the Trafalgar Square riot but their strategy of distancing themselves from any active opposition to the Tories meant that they lost the 1992 election.

Failure in British Government shows how even an apparently all-powerful government is vulnerable to mass opposition. Thatcher had a large majority, a loyal civil service and a weak opposition, but she still completely failed to introduce the poll tax. Arrogant to the last, she wrote in her memoirs about the poll tax, 'its benefits were just becoming apparent when it was abandoned'![9]

Thatcher's government dreamt up the poll tax apparently confident that they would not be opposed. In parliamentary terms, they were right. The book acknowledges that the only real opposition to the tax was the mass campaign outside parliament which was independent of the official labour movement and was successful in getting rid of both the poll tax and the prime minister. However, it is a major weakness of the book that the mass movement which had such an impact on the political situation is mentioned only in passing.

The poll tax was only one spectacular example of how Tory policies during the 1980s undermined the long term strength of their own organisation. Another crucial factor was the state of the economy. The economic recession of the early 1980s played a major part in undermining the morale and commitment of Tory members. The continuing economic decline of the 1990s has accelerated that process and created bitter divisions within the party.

Local party organisation continues to play a crucial role in election campaigns despite the growth of the mass media. The Conservatives would have lost the 1987 general election if they had abandoned campaigning at a local level.[10] The malaise in the Conservative Party organisation will therefore make it harder for them to win elections in the future. One possible salvation for the Tories lies with the Labour Party. Labour leader Tony Blair is following in Neil Kinnock's footsteps, driving Labour ever further towards the Tories, while the Tories themselves sink to new depths of unpopularity.

Notes

1 P Whiteley, P Seyd, J Richardson, *True Blues—the Politics of Conservative Party Membership* (Oxford University Press 1994), p96.
2 D Butler, A Adonis, T Travers, *Failure in British Government—the Politics of the Poll Tax* (Oxford University Press 1994), p 148.
3 Ibid, pp52-53.
4 P Whiteley, P Seyd, J Richardson, op cit, p169.
5 D Butler, A Adonis, T Travers, op cit, p249.
6 Ibid, p246.
7 Ibid, p155.
8 Ibid, p130.
9 Ibid, p183.
10 P Whiteley, P Seyd, J Richardson, op cit, p215.

Jazz: a reply to critics

CHARLIE HORE

In the early 1930s Kansas City jazz musicians began a tradition known as the 'cutting contest', where they tried to outdo each other in stamina and inventiveness, the losers being humiliated off the stage. Mike Hobart and Dave Harker seem to have adopted that tradition in their replies to my 'Jazz—a People's Music?'[1] Cutting contests seemingly made for great music; whether they are a useful form for cultural discussion seems to me doubtful.

My article began by quoting Trotsky: 'Marxism alone can explain how and why a given tendency in art has originated in a given period of history.' Matt Kelly, in his reply, quite correctly noted that '...Trotsky was not suggesting that this had already been done, but rather that it was a task that as yet awaited attention.' My original article aimed to do that for jazz in a brief and polemical sketch of jazz history and its relationship to other black American musical forms, a format that necessarily makes for a great deal of simplification and omissions. To find myself accused of '...a deep pessimism for the present, a depiction of a previous golden age and a retreat into Third Worldism' (Hobart, p145) and '...in danger of making unnecessary concessions to black nationalism and separatism...' (Harker, p148) is less than heartening.

Taking up every point in three very different replies is impossible in the short space available to me. What I intend to do here is take up two themes that run through the three articles: (i) the arguments about jazz history and its direcion today; (ii) the more important political arguments about black American history and culture.

All my critics focused on two supposed major errors in 'Jazz—a people's music?': 'the idea of some "golden age" of 'jazz' containing some undefined essence which then got 'watered down', co-opted, commoditised...' (Harker, p149)[2]; and the idea that I somehow privileged jazz as *the* popular music of American black ghettos.

The second point can be dealt with summarily. I focused on jazz and its popularity because that was the subject of my article, and thus I necessarily paid less attention to other black musical forms. But I explicitly argued that 'Jazz was a form of black musical expression, but not always the most important or the most popular one' and that '...jazz cannot be understood in isolation from other forms of American black music.'

As to the 'golden age' argument, it's true that I think jazz today is less innovative and less important in terms of popular music overall than it was 30 years ago. It is hard to find a jazz writer who disagrees with this truism.[3] But this is quite different from seeing jazz as having had some 'golden age' of authenticity which became contaminated by commercialism. I argued at some length in my original article against the artificial separation between 'authentic' and 'commercial' made by Eric Hobsbawm in *The Jazz Scene*, which I see as a consequence of Hobsbawm's Stalinist politics.[4] Instead I attempted to explain the history of jazz as a musical form with a built in drive to innovate and diversify, to understand the strengths and weaknesses of different moments in its evolution, and to relate this to changes in black American life.

There is no simple formula to express this. Mike Hobart is quite wrong, for instance, to suggest that jazz has always been an expression of black militancy—there is no trace of this in the vast majority of the jazz of the 1920s and 1930s, for instance. Nor is it the case that the 'new jazz' of the early 1960s was any less innovative than, say, swing or bebop. It is true, however, that the explicit political commitment of the 'new jazz' coincided with a marked decrease in its popularity among black listeners.[5] I attempted to explain this by pointing to the ways in which soul music reflected[6] the growing confidence and militancy among black Americans in the early 1960s, and in particular the fact that soul music allowed the voicing of explicit protest and anger. If my critics have a different explanation for this undoubted fact, they failed to spell it out.

This is a political judgement, not a musical one. I argued that '...the new jazz produced some of the most moving and profound jazz ever.' But from the late 1960s onwards jazz went into a decline from which it has not yet recovered, in part because of the rise of newer forms of black musical expression, and I concluded that 'it is important not to mourn this, or pretend that it's not happened, but to understand why.'

Mike Hobart's challenge to this begins with a singularly distorted summary of my argument, and then questions the idea of jazz being in decline: 'the last 20 years of jazz have not been anything like as catastrophic as the period between 1929 and 1935, which virtually eliminated existing jazz forms, or the period of 1947 to 1953...' (Hobart, p142).

Now this is a quite astonishing comparison to make, if we are talking about musical development and innovation. The period 1929 to 1935 saw the development in Kansas City of the swing style which was to become *the* popular music in the USA of the late 1930s,[7] while the period 1947 to 1953 saw the explosive growth and development of bebop. The majority of Charlie Parker's greatest records, for instance, were cut during that period. And 'catastrophic' was certainly not the word that Miles Davis would have used to describe the period:

> *To have experienced 52nd Street* [the Manhattan street where most of New York's jazz clubs were located] *between 1945 and 1949 was like reading a textbook to the future of music... You had Art Tatum, Tiny Grimes, Red Allen, Dizzy* [Gillespie], *Bird* [Charlie Parker], *Bud Powell,* [Thelonious] *Monk all down there on that one street sometimes on the same night.*[8]

Mike is here confusing artistic innovation and development with the health of the jazz economy. It's true that the working opportunities for jazz musicians today are greater than they were in the two periods he refers to, but that says nothing about the vitality of the music itself. I began my article by suggesting that there was a contradiction between the popularity of jazz and its creative decline—Mike's arguments about the health of the economy merely serve to underline that.

Of course there has been innovation in jazz over the past 20 years—my argument concerns the scale and influence of the innovations. Mike concedes that no musician of the status of Charlie Parker or John Coltrane has appeared in this period, but fails to see that this is linked to the wider decline of the music. Great musicians do not spring fully formed from the womb—precisely because of the nature of jazz as a collective music their development depends on a community of musicians from whom they learn. It is because there have been no fundamentally innovative *schools* of jazz in the last 20 years that there have been no great musicians springing from them.

His explanation for the decline of jazz in the early 1960s is equally unconvincing. 'Free' jazz was by the early 1960s abandoning (or being abandoned by) the jazz clubs for simple economic reasons, as a musician who played with the avant-garde pianist Cecil Taylor explained:

> [Taylor's music] *is completely unsaleable in the nightclubs because of the fact that each composition lasts, or could last, an hour and a half. Bar owners aren't interested in this, because if there's one thing they hate to see it's a bunch of people sitting around open-mouthed with their brains absolutely paralysed by the music.*[9]

Incidentally, it wasn't true by the early 1960s that most jazz clubs were located in black areas, still less that they were closed for years by black uprisings, the majority of which lasted less than a week.

The second strand of Mike's argument about the record companies equally confuses cause and effect. The big record companies had no more intrinsic interest in Led Zeppelin than they did in jazz—they just saw more money in rock. Where they thought they could still make money out of jazz artists they continued to record and promote their music. For instance, three months before John Coltrane died, he signed a two year contract with Impulse! Records for a $40,000 a year advance.[10] And when in the mid-1980s the record companies detected a revival in interest in jazz, they began a massive programme of re-releasing old material, with no more knowledge of, or interest in, the music itself than they had had in the 1960s.

Finally, Mike's arguments about the popularity of jazz (echoed in part by Dave Harker) essentially say that jazz was never more than a minority taste anyway, as it is today, so that nothing has really changed. In part there is a confusion about what 'mass' popularity really means. I'll suggest the (admittedly imprecise) definition that 'mass' culture is that which enters into the everyday lives of most people. On that definition, jazz had a mass audience for most of its history. Here, for instance, is Malcolm X on Lansing, Michigan (a city of less than 100,000 people), and Boston in the 1930s:

> [in black bars and restaurants] *The jukeboxes were wailing Erskine Hawkins' 'Tuxedo Junction', Slim and Slam's 'Flatfoot Floogie', things like that. Sometimes, big bands from New York, out touring the one-night stands in the sticks, would play for big dances in Lansing. Everybody with legs would come out to see any performer who bore the magic name 'New York'.*
>
> *Jukeboxes blared Erskine Hawkins, Duke Ellington, Cootie Williams, dozens of others... The biggest bands, like these, played at the Roseland State ballroom...one night for Negroes, the next for whites.*[11]

The pianist Clifford Jordan similarly remembers the South Side of Chicago in the late 1940s:

Yeah, all the jukeboxes, they had jazz, but nobody called it 'jazz' then. It was just music. It was just our music, folk music...it was just easy to come by the music. They had two or three key record stores in the neighbourhood.[12]

And in *Hard Bop* David Rosenthal argued that:

From 1945 to 1965, jazz attracted the ghetto's most gifted young musicians. During the late 1950s and early 1960s, hard bop was the basic idiom in the neighbourhoods where such youngsters lived... In 1959, virtually every apartment building in areas like Harlem or the South Side of Chicago housed at least a few knowledgable, serious jazz fans...[13]

The above should be enough to disprove Dave Harker's assertion that jazz was 'made by professionals for a *tiny* percentage of the record buying public—and a largely white, male, college educated minority at that' (Harker, p151),[14] as well as Mike Hobart's claim that '...at no stage has innovative jazz been anything remotely close to a mass music' (Hobart, p143). Figures about record sales simply miss the point. In 1929 the only way to hear Bessie Smith was to buy a record or wait until she played live near to where you lived. From sometime in the mid-1930s onwards most jazz was probably listened to on jukeboxes or radios, rather than live or on individuals' record players, though live performances remained important.

Two subsidiary points flow from this. The first is that, although jazz was indeed a creature of 'the era of mass reproduction', most jazz was still listened to collectively (dancehall audiences, customers in bars and juke-joints, families or groups of friends around radios, etc). The second is that the notion of a specialist 'jazz audience' who only listen for preference to one form of music is an inappropriate way to understand the position of jazz in black Americans' everyday lives. Jazz was one musical form among many available on jukeboxes, the radio and in record shops. Whether most black Americans who were interested in music listened primarily to jazz, or rhythm 'n blues, or country blues, or any other musical form is an unanswerable and irrelevant question. The real point is that from the late 1920s to sometime in the mid-1960s it was an integral part of black American musical culture.

This brings me to the argument about exactly what constitutes 'black American culture' and the related arguments about the importance of the experience of racism and resistance in the formation of jazz and other black American musical forms.[15] For Mike Hobart, 'Charlie's main problem is that he sees race as the only motor in the history of jazz's development' (Hobart, p145). Now of course I never said that: my article aimed to explain the development of jazz *both* in terms of the internal logic of the music which led to new forms and styles *and* in relation to changes in black American lives and expectations. In that context race (and struggles against racial oppression) were fundamentally important motors for cultural change.

Mike goes on to say that '...slavery, segregation, and the racism they produced are an integral feature of capitalist development and therefore cannot be separated from it' (Hobart, p145). This is true enough, but precisely because oppression is used to divide the working class, it affects different groups of workers in different ways. Racial oppression is a product of capitalist exploitation, but that does not mean that it can be *reduced* to exploitation.

Yet that is essentially what Mike argues, insisting that the 'interference of capital' was essentially colour blind and that the isolation of jazz musicians from their audience was just caused by a specialised division of labour. The simple fact, however, is that the everyday experience of racism created a much greater bond between black American musicians and their audiences, in part because, however much the musicians may have wanted to distance themselves from their origins, there was (until the late 1960s) very little space for them to do it in.

Jazz musicians touring the southern USA, for instance, regularly slept in the homes of their audiences, simply because there was no black hotel in the town, while many New York jazz clubs refused to serve as patrons the jazz musicians who played there. Mary Wells vividly described coming up against the limitations forced on all black performers by racism:

> *It was in New Orleans, and I wasn't thinking. You know, the Martin Luther King trip was well on the road and all... I started drinking out of this water fountain, and all these people started lookin' at me. And me, so much a fool, I say to myself, 'Oh, they know who I am, I'm Mary Wells.' Then I look up and see the sign. Yeah, you got it. WHITES ONLY. Me in my little Motown star bubble. All of a sudden everything kind of crushes.*[16]

Yet the closeness between performers and audiences cannot only be explained by the performers' inability to distance themselves from everyday racism. One defining feature of all black American musical forms is the emphasis on expressing shared feelings and emotions, on 'telling it like it is'. And I'd argued that this emphasis is a function, at least in part, of the experience of racism. In a society which denies your humanity, to express openly feelings of love, hate, rage, pain, sexual longing and jealousy is to assert that humanity: 'If you prick me, do I not bleed?'

And one of the key motors for change in black American music has been the shift from taking racism as given to openly challenging it. As Big Bill Broonzy pithily explained in the early 1960s, 'Young people have forgotten how to cry the blues. Now they talk and get lawyers'.[17]

All musical forms are contradictory, and can be used to carry a wide variety of messages. The blues asserts humanity as well as advocating resignation. Gospel music, often seen as the ultimate expression of powerlessness, became an essential mobiliser and organiser in the Civil Rights Movement, which built in turn on earlier black struggles. Steel workers in Birmingham, Alabama, for instance used gospel quartets in union organising drives in the 1930s and 1940s.[18]

Soul music, which grew out of a combination of gospel forms and secular lyrics, marked a fundamental change in black American music, which corresponded to a fundamental shift in expectations. The very tone of the music was upbeat, brash and confident, even when dealing with purely personal topics. Many purists in the 1960s dismissed soul music (at least in its Tamla Motown form) as 'watered down for white consumption', and Mike Hobart echoes their arguments. Yet this is a fundamental misunderstanding of what soul music represented. For the first time ever black artists gained mass white audiences by taking the basic harmonies of gospel and doo-wop music and adding a compelling, non-stop and above all very loud dance beat to it. Certainly to audiences at the time, it sounded anything but 'diluted'. (John Lennon reportedly once asked one of the Four Tops, 'When you cats go into the studio, what does the drummer beat on to get that backbeat? You use a bloody *tree* or something?')[19]

Now of course Berry Gordy did not do this as a contribution to the struggle against racism. He was in it for the money, and could be as vicious as any white record company boss. And soul music could as equally be used to promote the ideas of 'black capitalism', of accommodation within the system, as it could express the hopes and aspirations of black workers. But this should simply serve as a reminder that no cultural form is inherently progressive or revolutionary—their uses, meanings and limitations are ultimately defined politically, and people interpret them in the light of their own experiences and expectations.

All of the above should, I hope, disprove Dave Harker's assertion that I see the '"black American experience" [as] somehow monolithic and non-contradictory…' (Harker, p148). But I do want to deal in more detail with some of his arguments, which seem almost to give up on any attempt to locate culture in historical contexts.

Dave begins his reply by questioning the validity of concepts such as 'the black American experience' and 'black music', arguing that they properly belong to black nationalist rather than socialist theory. He is of course quite right to point out that all too often these ideas are used by black nationalists in ahistorical and essentialist ways which serve to distort the class differences that divide the 'black community'. These arguments have been refuted in detail by previous articles in this journal, and I do not intend to rework them here.[20]

But just because these concepts are often misused does not prove them wrong; it rather means that we are engaged in a struggle over their meaning. I want to argue that, provided we understand them as historically specific terms, both concepts are essential to understanding jazz and other modern American musical forms.

What I mean by the shorthand term 'the black American experience' is that chattel slavery and post-slavery institutionalised racism produced a set of life experiences (and strategies for dealing with them) that were *fundamentally similar* for the vast majority of black people across the USA. Out of those experiences the slaves created a culture, a way of life, with distinctive forms of religion, customs, morals and musics which drew on both the dominant cultures of Southern whites, and the many diverse African cultures from which the slaves had been plundered.

After the abolition of slavery in 1865 the brief freedoms of Reconstruction were buried under the structures of Jim Crow which, in the Southern United States (where 75 percent of the black population lived until the Second World War), reinforced that culture through a near total segregation of everyday social life. (In Birmingham, Alabama, for instance, a 1930 by-law made it illegal for blacks and whites to play dominoes or draughts 'together or in company with one another').[21] Class divisions among blacks,[22] as well as the differences between the Southern states and elsewhere, made for vast differences in the everyday experience and extent of racism. But the fact remains that for the vast majority of black Americans racism was (and is) a fundamental limiting factor in their lives, despite the increase in the size of the black middle class since the 1960s.

The shared culture that arose out of those experiences was a complex, contradictory and above all dynamic one that defies any simplistic analysis, and all I attempted in my original article was a brief sketch of it. Eugene Genovese's summary of the evolution of black American religion acts as a useful warning against one dimensional interpretations of that culture, as well as a definition of it:

> *Even so brief a sketch warns of two major pitfalls in the evaluation of the religion...the facile tendency to assume that the Southern slaves passively*

absorbed a religion handed down from above and completely relinquished their African heritage without replacing it with anything new; and the mechanistic error of assuming that religion either sparked the slaves to rebellion or rendered them docile...it did display the same creative impulse to blend ideas from diverse sources into the formulation of a world-view sufficently complex to link acceptance of what had to be endured with a determined resistance to the pressures for despair and dehumanisation.[23]

It seems to me that black musical forms expressed that same complexity of world view, evolving as the opportunities for resistance became ever greater. We can only begin to understand jazz, blues, gospel (and for that matter, rap, hip-hop and jungle today)[24] if we grasp their origins as musics played by black artists for black audiences who shared the same fundamental life experiences and expectations.

Music by its very nature is a highly permeable art form, and there was a constant two way trading of influences between black and white Americans. Blues and jazz musicians borrowed all the time from white musicians, just as white musicians borrowed from them. (The key difference was that while black musicians were prepared to acknowledge this, the same was rarely true for the whites.) Nevertheless, black musical forms retained direct African traits and influences until well into the 1940s. The musicologist Alan Lomax commented on a song that he recorded in Mississippi in 1941:

Years later Roswell Rudd discovered a virtual match for Tangle Eye's holler in a recording from Senegal, an important source for African slaves. When we intercut these two pieces on a tape, it sounded as if Tangle Eye and the Senegalese were answering each other, phrase by phrase.[25]

In this context the argument of the musicologist Philip Tagg, quoted by both Dave Harker and Matt Kelly, about the presence in other musical traditions of such traits as 'blue notes' and call and response, is simply irrelevant. Undoubtedly such traits can be found in many musical traditions. But it seems to me undeniable that the *specific* traits that went to distinguish blues and jazz came largely from African origins, from a culture that slaves and their descendants developed.

Finally, the above should explain why I used the term 'a people's music' to define jazz (and why it could usefully be extended to other black American forms). It is of the essence of jazz that it was created by poor black urban Americans, not handed down by the bourgeoisie, and that it carried within it a refusal to accept the limitations of racism. Today, of course, it is impossible to divide all American music into what is 'black' and what is 'white'; many black artists make a living playing almost entirely to white audiences (Diana Ross, Michael

Jackson and Sonny Rollins, to name but three), while it is expected that white rock musicians acknowledge the influences that blues and soul have had on them. That blurring of differences reflects fundamental changes in black American lives brought about principally by their own struggles.

It also reflects what is arguably one of the most important cultural shifts of the 20th century: the fact that the majority of popular music across the Western world is ultimately derived from black American music. The evolution of those musical forms from being 'people's musics' to mass produced commodities available to anyone who can afford a radio or a tape machine, is an enormous cultural gain, and one which I celebrated in my original article.

In the end, however, this is not simply an argument about history. If we want to understand the significance of rap, hip-hop, jungle and related musical forms today, we have to begin by understanding that they arose in the same way as jazz and blues; music created for working class black Americans by working class black Americans. As Alan Lomax noted:

> [The blues] *arose in a period much like our own. Our species has never been more powerful and wealthy, nor more ill at ease. Homeless and desperate people in America live in the shadow of undreamed-of productivity and luxury... Rage and anxiety pervade the emotions and the actions of both the haves and have-nots. And the sound of the worried blues of the old Delta is heard in back alleys and palaces, alike.*[26]

Yet history is not simply repeating itself. Where the blues was a music of accommodation, the dominant tone of modern black music is refusal and rebellion. It can be co-opted, it can reinforce divisons inside the working class as well as break them down, and it does not automatically lead to revolutionary conclusions—no music does. But the fact that it has reached mass international audiences tells us that the rage and anger it articulates are felt by workers across the world.

Notes

1 *International Socialism* 61. The replies, by Mike Hobart, Dave Harker and Matt Kelly, appeared in *International Socialism* 64. All further references to my original article and the replies will be given in the text.

2 The quote 'watered down' is from my original article, where I referred specifically to the boom in white musicians recording 'jazz' in the 1920s. Anyone who doubts that this *specific form* wasn't 'watered down' for white consumption should listen to the early recordings of Paul Whiteman or consider his stated aim at his first major concert in 1924: '[to show the] advance which had been made in popular music from the day of discordant early jazz to the

melodious forms of the present.' Quoted in B Sidran, *Black Talk* (New York, 1981), p69.

3 See, for instance, the introduction to D Rosenthal, *Hard Bop* (New York, 1993): 'No one would cite the jazz of the last 15 years as an example of healthy evolution…' (pxi).

4 Originally published under the pseudonym Francis Newton (London, 1963) and reissued with minor changes under Hobsbawm's own name (London, 1990). (Hobsbawm, incidentally, is not consistently guilty of this: the last chapter largely consists of an attack on the 'golden age' theory.) Both Dave Harker and Matt Kelly attack me for using Hobsbawm and Sidney Finkelstein's *Jazz: A People's Music* (New York, 1948) as a basis for my arguments, because they were Stalinists. As it happens, I never mentioned Finkelstein's book in my original article, because it was unavailable at the time. While there are problems with both books, which do derive from the authors' Stalinist politics, both are valuable as attempts to apply a materialist analysis to jazz and to insist on the importance of jazz in modern musical history. Dave Harker's offhand dismissal of both brings the words 'babies' and 'bathwater' forcibly to mind.

5 For an analysis of the decline of blues music's popularity, see M Haralambos, *Right On: from Blues to Soul in Black America* (Ormskirk, 1994).

6 Dave Harker laid great stress on demolishing this metaphor, arguing that 'reflection' implies a purely mechanical correspondence between social change and cultural change. Now of course any metaphor will fall apart if too much weight is put on it, but I used it simply to stress that cultural changes were ultimately determined by social changes, or, as Marx put it: 'Being determines consciousness'. I fail to see that his preferred term 'correspondence' says anything very different.

7 As I noted in my original article, by 1939 85 percent of all records sold in the USA were swing recordings.

8 M Davis and Q Troupe, *Miles—the Autobiography* (London, 1992), p88.

9 B Neidlinger, quoted in F Kovsky, *Black nationalism and the revolution in music* (New York, 1970), p147.

10 J C Thomas, *Chasin' the Trane* (New York, 1985), p222.

11 Malcolm X, *The Autobiography of Malcolm X* (London 1968), pp108, 116.

12 Quoted in D Rosenthal, op cit, p69.

13 Ibid, pp62-63.

14 Dave gives no less than five references to Eric Hobsbawm's *The Jazz Scene* to back up this assertion. However, on two of the pages he refers to there is no discussion of the jazz audience, and on the other three Hobsbawm makes it clear that he is only talking about the white audience in America.

15 Matt Kelly is quite right to point out that similar processes of cultural interaction took place in Southern America and the Caribbean, and that these added to the musical influences available to black musicians in the USA (Kelly, p154). Lack of space in my original article prevented any consideration of these traditions.

16 Quoted in G Hershey, *Nowhere to Run* (London, 1985), p144.

17 Quoted in M Haralambos, op cit, p82.

18 G Lipsitz, *Rainbow at Midnight—Labor and Culture in the 1940s* (Urbana, Illinois, 1994), pp303-304.

19 Quoted in G Hershey, op cit, p186.

20 See A Shawki, 'Black liberation and socialism in the United States', *International Socialism* 47, and A Callinicos, 'Race and Class', *International Socialism* 55.

21 Quoted in M Marable, *Race, Reform and Rebellion* (Jackson, Mississippi, 1984), p10.

22 For an account of class divisions among American blacks even during slavery, see A Shawki, op cit.

23 E D Genovese, *Roll, Jordan, Roll* (New York, 1976), p183.
24 For an excellent account of the origins of rap and hip-hop music, see B Cross, *It's Not About a Salary…* (London, 1994).
25 A Lomax, *The Land Where the Blues Began* (London, 1994), p276.
26 Ibid, px.

Bookwatch: Ireland

PAT RIORDAN

Over the last few months great changes have taken place in Irish society. The ceasefire in Northern Ireland seems to have drawn to a close an entire era of politics in the North. The underlying causes of violence still remain—the existence of the Northern Irish state and the maintenance of the British army in the North—but the ceasefire does offer a real challenge to socialists. An opening has been created that socialist forces can seek to fill by building an alternative to the ideas of Unionism and Nationalism.

To understand what is taking place in the North, and the political forces involved, it helps to have an alternative to the often misleading coverage of events which dominates the British and Irish media. There is a whole industry of literature covering not only the events in Northern Ireland over the last 25 years, but also the history of Britain's involvement in Ireland. A number of these books are very helpful for a fuller understanding of the situation now unfolding in the six counties.[1]

Most people wanting to tackle events in Ireland will wish to begin in the 20th century. The best place to start is the period 1916-1921. Prior to 1916 John Redmond, the leading constitutional nationalist of his day, introduced a Home Rule for Ireland Bill to the British parliament. The bill generated immense popular support in Ireland and was meant to enter the British statute books once the First World War was over. The bill, however, caused a major crisis in Irish politics. In the North, Edward Carson, the godfather of modern Ulster Unionism, raised a force of Ulster volunteers to fight against the bill. Nationalists from both the constitutional and the physical force traditions joined together with a number of labour organisations to form the Irish Volunteers with the purpose of defending Home Rule or fighting for it if it wasn't granted. The British government played a double game, inducing both Ulster and Irish volunteers to join the army, with promises of a satisfactory settlement for each at the end of the hostilities.

Against this background the volunteers under the leadership of anti-Redmond Republicans seized the post office and other strategic points in Dublin at Easter 1916. The Irish rebellion had begun— the Easter Uprising led to the genesis of the modern Republican movement. After the uprising an irregular army (the IRA), and an illegal Irish parliament (Dail Eireann) were established. British irregular forces, the auxiliaries and the Black and Tans, were brought in. A vicious and bloody war ensued. Summary execution by the British forces of both the 'rebels' and non-combatants was the norm and entire areas were looted, sacked and burnt. The period is covered in many books, a good descriptive introduction being Ulick O'Connor's *The Troubles*.[2] The best books, however, are by the combatants themselves. In particular read Tom Barry's *Guerilla Days in Ireland*[3] and Ernie O'Malley's *On Another Man's Wound*.[4] Both books give a real feel of the events and the bloody nature of the Tan war, and also give insights into the kind of people who made up the Irish Republican Army. Generally volunteers were from either a farming or a college background, wholly patriotic in outlook and usually disdainful of politics.

The Republicans eventually signed a peace treaty with the British in 1921, which granted Home Rule status within Southern Ireland and ensured partition. The settlement led to a split in the Republican movement, between the pro-treaty 'Freestaters' and the anti-treaty Republicans. The treaty led not only to a civil war, but also to the development of bourgeois states, both north and south of the border. Much of the literature covering the civil war and the development of the Southern Irish state is little more than a defence of the Southern state. Two of the most interesting books covering the period, Tim Pat Coogan's recent biographies of Michael Collins and Eamon de Valera,[5] fall into this tradition. Collins was a brilliant guerilla leader and IRA hero of the Tan war, but was also the man who signed the treaty with the British. As a result he has always held a rather contradictory position in the Republican pantheon. De Valera, on the other hand, was the leader of the Republican forces in the civil war, but after the end of the civil war broke with the Republicans and formed Fianna Fail as a constitutional party. De Valera and his party were to dominate Southern Irish politics for the next 50 years. De Valera was capable of using radical sounding rhetoric while being profoundly conservative.

He was one of the chief architects of the Southern state, and was the darling of the Catholic Church. Both De Valera and Collins, whatever their differences, were at times bourgeois revolutionaries and nationalistic political figures. Both biographies are worth reading, not only for the importance of their main characters, but also for the detail and background they give to the civil war and events after it. Also worth a critical reading is C Desmond Greaves's *Liam Mellowes and the Irish Revolution*,[6] one of the first books about a more left wing figure from the anti-treaty IRA. However, Greaves comes from the old Irish Communist Party tradition which argues that the Republican movement is the key vehicle for radical social change, so he portrays Mellowes as some sort of semi-conscious communist. This is simply wishful thinking. A significant left wing current did not develop within Republicanism until the 1930s and even then it was a wholly minority tradition.

To understand the major events and movements in modern Ireland, we also have to look at developments in Northern Ireland. The Northern state was sectarian from its conception in 1921. The North had suffered the highest number of deaths in the Tan war and the civil war, and the state began in a wave of pogroms. These beginnings are dealt with most fully in Michael Farrell's *The Orange State*[7] and Geoffrey Bell's *The Protestants of Ulster*.[8] Both books are important works and both are written from a left wing perspective. Both, however, share a fatal flaw. Bell and Farrell accept the idea, common on the left, of the Protestant working class as a homogenous and reactionary mass. Protestant workers, they argue, constitute a 'labour aristocracy'. This argument has long given a left cover to the Republican movement's dismissive attitude towards Protestant workers. Gerry Adams, for example, adopted the same argument wholesale in his own writings.[9]

This argument is no longer viable. Unionism today is in crisis. The Unionist tradition of tying Protestant worker to Protestant boss, and so dividing the working class, is increasingly untenable in a time of major economic recession. Under the weight of recession the old Unionist partnership, which was based upon being able to provide a job and a house (however bad the job and poor the house), is being cut apart. The legacy of Unionism lingers on, but the possibility of building an alternative to it out of the ceasefire is also very real. The strike in Derry over sectarian killings and the walkout at Harland and Wolff in Belfast last year show the openings of a socialist alternative to the stale game of Unionist politics. For a more optimistic picture than that offered by Farrell and Bell, readers should see *Can Protestant and Catholic Unite?* by Mark Hewitt.[10]

Also worth looking at is *The Irish Republican Congress* by George Gillmore[11] which is a handy antidote to the myth that Catholic and

Protestant have never fought side by side. The Republican Congress was a left split from the Republican movement that attracted a significant lay of Protestant workers. The nemesis of the Congress came with the 1934 march to Bodenstown, the Republican yearly pilgrimage for all sections of the IRA. The Protestant contingent of the march, carrying a left wing banner, was removed on the orders of the IRA leader McBride, for being 'too communistic', a telling reminder of the political limitations of Republicanism. A more complete account of campaigns in the same period is provided by Munck and Rolston's *Belfast in the Thirties: An Oral History,*[12] which tells the story of sectarian strife between Catholic and Protestant, and also of socialist organisation involving both.

Besides books about the development of the Northern state, there is a wealth of material dealing with the major paramilitary players on both sides. The major writer on the Loyalist death squads, the UVF and the UDA, is the journalist Martin Dillon. His books *The Shankill Butchers* and *Stone Cold*[13] deal with two of the most vicious Loyalist actions of the last 25 years. Dillon's books are well researched and contain a wealth of information about security forces, dirty tricks campaigns and army collusion in sectarian activity. They are fairly balanced, but don't expect any analysis. A book with a pro-British angle, but very useful nonetheless, is Don Anderson's *Fourteen May Days: The Inside Story of the Loyalist Strike of 1974*,[14] about the strike which brought down the power sharing assembly in 1974. The book is a timely reminder of how Loyalism, when it was strong, worked. The strike had little to do with picketing or workers' democracy. It was controlled by the UDA, the biggest Loyalist parliamentary group. The army and the security forces were openly sympathetic and dissident workers were frightened away from work by straightforward intimidation. It was one of the few purely reactionary strikes in history. It is worth remembering while reading the book that, although until the 1994 ceasefire the Loyalists were highly effective sectarian murder gangs, they no longer had the same power as they did in 1974.

The largest body of work concerning Northern Ireland deals in one way or another with the Provisional IRA. If the present phase of violence can be given a starting date it was probably 1966, when there were a wave of murders by the UVF. The modern IRA did not come into being properly until the late 1960s, against a background of sectarian killings, the civil rights movement and the introduction of British troops. The idea that the Provisionals were the architects of the violence of Northern Ireland is contradicted by the facts. On the issue of cold blooded murder by gangs of rampaging assassins in the North, readers should see Eamonn McCann's *Bloody Sunday in Derry—What Really Happened*,[15] a detailed account of the murder of 13 civilians by the British Parachute

Regiment in 1972. The book outlines the political strategy behind the killings and its repercussions for the people of Derry and the North.

The book that gives the best outline of the formation of the modern IRA is Bishop and O'Mallie's *The Provisional IRA*,[16] a not particularly sympathetic but thorough account of the Provisionals. Those wishing to balance it with a more partisan account should see Kevin Kelley's *The Longest War*.[17] The most comprehensive overview of the history of the Republicans up to 1979 is J Bowyer Bell's *The Secret Army: The IRA 1916-79*.[18] Another fine book, one particularly useful on the splits between left and right in the IRA, is Con Foley's *Legion of the Rearguard*.[19] On much the same subject, though more jaundiced, is Patterson's *The Politics of Illusion*,[20] which details the split at the onset of the Troubles between the Official and Provisional IRA. The Officials were formerly the more left wing of the two groupings, but their Dublin based leadership believed in a Stalinised 'solution' to the Irish question: first there would be general democratic reforms, then a national revolution, then at some future juncture socialism could be achieved. Of the two groups, the Provisionals picked up more support. In the early 1970s the Provisionals were firmly in the physical force tradition—derisive of 'politics' and 'political solutions', and committed wholly to militarism. An attempt to merge the formally leftward leaning politics of the Officials and the methodology of the Provisionals was made with the formation of the Irish National Liberation Army/Irish Republican Socialist Party. The organisation was the smaller brother of the Provos. It had a particularly extreme strain of Maoist politics. The failure of the organisation remains an object lesson in the impossibility of grafting socialist politics onto Republican organisation. The whole tragic business is dealt with in detail in Holland and McDonald's *INLA: Deadly Divisions*.[21]

By the early 1980s the main event affecting the broader Republican movement was the Long Kesh hunger strike of 1980-1981. The strike was an attempt to win back political status for Republican prisoners. David Beresford's *Ten Men Dead*[22] is a deeply moving account of the bravery and sacrifice of those involved. By the mid-1980s the Republican movement, on the back of the hunger strike and the electoral success that followed it, was attempting a move into official politics. The period 1981-1986 saw the growth of Sinn Fein in electoral terms, alongside an ongoing IRA military campaign, an approach summarised in the phrase, 'The armalite and the ballot box'.[23] The whole strategy is covered in detail in Liam Clarke's excellent book *Broadening the Battlefield*.[24] The growth of Sinn Fein floundered because, although the party had a solid base in the Catholic enclaves of the North, its vote never expanded beyond those immediate geographic boundaries. Sinn Fein has nothing to say to Protestant workers in the North, and little appeal for supporters of the 'mainstream' Social Democratic and Labour Party, which retains the allegiance of the majority of Northern Catholics, nor could it expand into the South on a purely North based ticket. The party's attitiude to social issues was tentative because it sought alliances with the pro-capitalist Fianna Fail, who it saw as 'fellow nationalists'. Fianna Fail was at the same time pushing through attacks on workers in the South, so Sinn Fein was compromised.

Major developments have not been confined to the North: significant changes have also occurred in Southern Irish politics. In electoral terms this has been shown in the growth of the vote for the Irish Labour Party. For the first time a class vote, albeit a distorted one, has become a factor in parliamentary politics. For a Marxist account of the Southern Labour Party, see Conor Costick's pamphlet *Why the Labour Party Fails*.[25] Successive Southern governments have been Northern Unionists' best advert for a divided Ireland but now Northern workers can look South and see not only a succession of weak and corrupt governments but also Southern workers' angry reaction to them. The resignation in 1994 of the Fianna Fail led coalition came amid a wave of scandals that exposed widescale corruption between church and state, chiefly the prime minister's attempt to cover up child sex abuse by members of the clergy. Some of the recent scandals and their effect on people's perception of the government is captured in Finton O'Toole's *Meanwhile Back at the Ranch*.[26]

In electoral terms the scandals have come to mean the swapping of one group of Tories, Fianna Fail, for another, Fine Gael. Yet Fine Gael's coalition and its Taoisoach (prime minister) John Bruton are, if anything, more unpopular than Fianna Fail. They gained office only by the willingness of smaller parties, including supposedly left wing ones such as the Democratic Left, to throw in their lot with them.

Still the left vote is only symptomatic of what is happening beyond and below parliamentary politics. As Kieran Allen argued in *International Socialism* 64,[27] there has been a sea change in the Southern working class. Like their British counterparts they have suffered years of 'new realism' preached by trade union leaders. These ideas now exist uneasily side by side with a growing anger and desire to fight amongst ordinary workers. There is also a general political mood that from time to time bursts into the open, the major recent example of this being around the X case and the issue of abortion. Movements like this, both political and industrial, have begun to blow away some of the stereotypes about Southern Ireland that are common in Northern Unionist circles, particularly the myth that all the people of the South are in thrall to the church.

Certainly the South has been a very conservative society. Yet the South also has a hidden history of struggle. In 1919, for instance,

Limerick had its own soviet (workers' council) and Limerick dairy workers bequeathed the workers' movement the immortal slogan, 'We make butter, not profits.' The period is covered in Liam Cahill's book *Limerick 1919: Forgotten Revolution*.[28] But the greatest single incident of working class militancy was the Dublin Lockout of 1913 when workers fought not only the employers but also the Catholic Church. The period is captured in Emmet Larkin's biography of the strike leader Jim Larkin,[29] James Plunkett's novel *Strumpet City*,[30] and more generally in Boyd's *Rise of the Irish Trade Unions*.[31] Jim Larkin was a major figure on the Irish left but, despite a formal commitment to the need of a revolutionary organisation, he never really escaped from his syndicalist background. His key role in the often forgotten Belfast dock strike of 1907, and that strike's role in uniting Catholic and Protestant workers are well captured in John Gray's *City in Revolt*.[32]

The modern Irish working class is still waiting for the political literature it deserves. But well worth reading is Roddy Doyle's marvellous *Barrytown Trilogy*.[33] His stories are deeply concerned with working class life. Populist, funny and compassionate, he is probably the premier descriptive writer in modern Ireland.

This article began by saying that the ceasefire offers a real opening for socialists. That there is a ceasefire, however, shouldn't really surprise us. Republican strategy and tactics, whether focusing on militarism or cutting deals with the British and Irish political establishment, flow from their nationalist politics. The Loyalist ceasefire may seem initially more confusing. But tactically Loyalism has often tail-ended Republicanism. The communities that the Loyalist gangs come from (and often prey on) are every bit as war weary as their Nationalist counterparts. To the traditions of the Republicans and Unionists, the working class, as a class, is marginal. A working class movement with socialist politics is a possibility that the Republicans ignore and Loyalists fear. But the North has seen mass movements, an especially important example being the civil rights movement of the late 1960s. The movement showed the possibility of a united fight for democratic changes spilling over into a fight for a different society. Highly recommended reading on this is Con McCluskey's *Off Our Knees*[34] but even better is Eamonn McCann's brilliant *War and an Irish Town*[35] The new edition, in particular, is essential reading for a socialist analysis of the North. The strength of the civil rights movement was that it was a mass movement. Its weakness was that it only developed 'on the march' an understanding of the limits of reform within the context of the Northern Irish state. The weakness of the left, particularly a genuine Marxist left, within the movement meant that the protests moved into the familiar channels of a constitutional nationalism and traditional Republicanism.

All the books I have mentioned are very useful and taken together give a fairly comprehensive picture of events and characters in modern Irish history. This alone, though, is not enough. The books I have mentioned are best read alongside some genuine Marxist works. For a critique of developments over the last 25 years and before, Chris Bambery's *Ireland's Permanent Revolution*[36] gives a solid and accessible outline. For a socialist analysis of modern Republicanism, readers should see Kieran Allen's pamphlet *Socialists, Republicans and the Armed Struggle*.[37] For a general Marxist understanding of the use of terrorism, Trotsky is unsurpassed. He ridicules the liberal idea of absolute moral concepts:

> *A slave owner who through cunning and violence shackles his slaves in chains, and a slave who through cunning and violence breaks the chains—let not the contemptible eunuchs tell us that they are equals before a court of morality.*[38]

While Trotsky draws a clear distinction between the violence between oppressor and oppressed, he also dismisses terrorist methods:

> *In our eyes individual terror is inadmissible precisely because it belittles the role of the masses in their own consciousness, reconciles them to their powerlessness, and turns their eyes and hopes toward a great avenger and liberator who someday will come and accomplish his mission.*[39]

Finally, any socialist interested in Ireland must read James Connolly's *Labour in Irish History*[40] or better still, indulge in a copy of his complete works.[41] Connolly was the leading Irish Marxist and his writings are wide ranging and very readable. Like all real figures, though, he was not flawless. Kieran Allen's *Politics of James Connolly*[42] is a political biography that is rewarding to read alongside Connolly himself. It provides a thorough analysis of Connolly's political virtues and limitations.

Notes

1 Beginning to tackle the subject of England's 800 year role in Ireland can seem daunting. A decent general overview, though by no means a Marxist analysis, is provided in R Kees, *The Green Flag,* 3 volumes (Penguin, 1987). Covering some of the same events, though from a more left wing standpoint, is T A Jackson, *Ireland Her Own* (Lawrence and Wishart, 1989).

2 U O'Connor, *The Troubles* (Mandarin, 1989).

3 T Barry, *Guerilla Days in Ireland* (Brandon, 1992).

4 E O'Malley, *On Another Man's Wound* (Anvil, 1992).

5 T P Coogan, *Michael Collins* (Metheun, 1991); *Eamonn De Valera* (Methuen, 1994).

6 C Desmond Greaves, *Liam Mellowes and the Irish Revolution* (Lawrence and Wishart, 1989).
7 M Farrell, *The Orange State* (Pluto Press, various ed).
8 G Bell, *The Protestants of Ulster* (Pluto Press, 1989).
9 G Adams, *The Politics of Irish Freedom* (Brandon, 1986).
10 M Hewitt, *Can Protestant and Catholic Unite?* (SWM Publications, 1993).
11 G Gilmore, *The Irish Republican Congress* (Cork Press, 1985).
12 R Munck and B Rolston, *Belfast in the Thirties: An Oral History* (Blackstaff Press, 1987).
13 M Dillon, *The Shankill Butchers* (Methuen, 1989).
14 D Anderson, *Fourteen May Days* (Gill & McMillan, 1994).
15 E McCann, M Sheils and B Hannigan *Bloody Sunday in Derry—What Really Happened* (Poolbeg, 1992).
16 Bishop and O'Mallie, *The Provisional IRA* (Corgi, 1987).
17 K Kelley, *The Longest War* (Zed Books, 1984).
18 J Bowyer Bell, *The Secret Army: The IRA 1916-1979* (Poolbeg, 1990).
19 C Foley, *Legion of the Rearguard* (Radius, 1990).
20 H Patterson, *The Politics of Illusion* (Radius, 1989).
21 Holland and McDonald, *INLA: Deadly Divisions* (Torc Publishers, 1994).
22 D Beresford, *Ten Men Dead* (Pluto Press, 1987).
23 D Morrison. The phrase comes from a speech at the Sinn Fein *Ard Fheis* (conference), 1983.
24 L Clarke, *Broadening the Battlefield* (Gill & McMillan, 1987).
25 C Costick, *Why the Labour Party Fails* (SWM Publications, 1993).
26 F O'Toole, *Meanwhile Back at the Ranch* (Dublin, 1994).
27 K Allen, 'What's Changing in Ireland?', (*International Socialism* 64, Autumn, 1994).
28 L Cahill, *Limerick 1919: Forgotten Revolution* (O'Brien Press, 1990).
29 E Larkin, *Jim Larkin—Irish Labour Leader* (Pluto Press, 1990).
30 J Plunkett, *Strumpet City* (Sphere, 1985).
31 A Boyd, *The Rise of the Irish Trade Unions* (Brandon, 1984).
32 J Gray, *City in Revolt* (Blackstaff Press, 1987).
33 R Doyle, *The Barrytown Trilogy* (Methuen, 1993).
34 C McCluskey, *Off Our Knees* (Poolbeg, 1989).
35 E McCann, *War and an Irish Town* (Pluto Press, 1993).
36 C Bambery, *Ireland's Permanent Revolution* (Bookmarks, 1986).
37 K Allen, *Socialists, Republicans and the Armed Stuggle* (SWM Publications, 1991).
38 L Trotsky, *Their Morals and Ours* (New Park, 1974).
39 L Trotsky, *Against Individual Terrorism* (Pathfinder, 1987).
40 J Connolly, *Labour in Irish History* (Bookmarks, 1988).
41 J Connolly, *Complete Works*, 2 volumes (New Book Publications, 1990).
42 K Allen, *The Politics of James Connolly* (Pluto Press, 1990).

The Socialist Workers Party is one of an international grouping of socialist organisations:

AUSTRALIA: International Socialists, GPO Box 1473N, Melbourne 3001

BELGIUM: Socialisme International, Rue Lovinfosse 60, 4030 Grivengée, Belgium

BRITAIN: Socialist Workers Party, PO Box 82, London E3

CANADA: International Socialists, PO Box 339, Station E, Toronto, Ontario M6H 4E3

CYPRUS: Ergatiki Demokratia, PO Box 7280, Nicosia

DENMARK: Internationale Socialister, Postboks 642, 2200 København N, Denmark

FRANCE: Socialisme International, BP 189, 75926 Paris Cedex 19

GERMANY: Sozialistische Arbeitergruppe, Postfach 180367, 60084 Frankfurt 1

GREECE: Organosi Sosialisliki Epanastasi, c/o Workers Solidarity, PO Box 8161, Athens 100 10, Greece

HOLLAND: International Socialists, PO Box 9720, 3506 GR Utrecht

IRELAND: Socialist Workers Movement, PO Box 1648, Dublin 8

NEW ZEALAND:
International Socialist Organization, PO Box 6157, Dunedin, New Zealand

NORWAY: Internasjonale Socialisterr, Postboks 5370, Majorstua, 0304 Oslo 3

POLAND: Solidarność Socjalistyczna, PO Box 12, 01-900 Warszawa 118

SOUTH AFRICA:
International Socialists of South Africa, PO Box 18530, Hillbrow 2038, Johannesburg

UNITED STATES:
International Socialist Organisation, PO Box 16085, Chicago, Illinois 60616

ZIMBABWE:
International Socialists, PO Box 6758, Harare

The following issues of *International Socialism* (second series) are available price £3.00 (including postage) from IS Journal, PO Box 82, London E3 3LH. *International Socialism* 2:58 and 2:65 are available on cassette from the Royal National Institute for the Blind (Peterborough Library Unit), Tel 01733 370777.

International Socialism 2:65 Special issue
Lindsey German: Frederick Engels: life of a revolutionary ★ John Rees: Engels' Marxism ★ Chris Harman: Engels and the origins of human society ★ Paul McGarr: Engels and natural science ★

International Socialism 2:64 Autumn 1994
Chris Harman: The prophet and the proletariat ★ Kieran Allen: What is changing in Ireland ★ Mike Haynes: The wrong road on Russia ★ Rob Ferguson: Hero and villain ★ Jane Elderton: Suffragette style ★ Chris Nineham: Two faces of modernism ★ Mike Hobart, Dave Harker and Matt Kelly: Three replies to 'Jazz—a people's music?' ★ Charlie Kimber: Bookwatch: South Africa—the struggle continues ★

International Socialism 2:63 Summer 1994
Alex Callinicos: Crisis and class struggle in Europe today ★ Duncan Blackie: The United Nations and the politics of imperialism ★ Brian Manning: The English Revolution and the transition from feudalism to capitalism ★ Lee Sustar: The roots of multi-racial labour unity in the United States ★ Peter Linebaugh: Days of villainy: a reply to two critics ★ Dave Sherry: Trotsky's last, greatest struggle ★ Peter Morgan: Geronimo and the end of the Indian wars ★ Dave Beecham: Ignazio Silone and *Fontamara* ★ Chris Bambery: Bookwatch: understanding fascism ★

International Socialism 2:62 Spring 1994
Sharon Smith: Mistaken identity—or can identity politics liberate the oppressed? ★ Iain Ferguson: Containing the crisis—crime and the Tories ★ John Newsinger: Orwell and the Spanish Revolution ★ Chris Harman: Change at the first millenium ★ Adrian Budd: Nation and empire—Labour's foreign policy 1945-51 ★ Gareth Jenkins: Novel questions ★ Judy Cox: Blake's revolution ★ Derek Howl: Bookwatch: the Russian Revolution ★

International Socialism 2:61 Winter 1994
Lindsey German: Before the flood? ★ John Molyneux: The 'politically correct' controversy ★ David McNally: E P Thompson—class struggle and historical materialism ★ Charlie Hore: Jazz—a people's music ★ Donny Gluckstein: Revolution and the challenge of labour ★ Charlie Kimber: Bookwatch: the Labour Party in decline ★

International Socialism 2:60 Autumn 1993
Chris Bambery: Euro-fascism: the lessons of the past and present tasks ★ Chris Harman: Where is capitalism going? (part 2) ★ Mike Gonzalez: Chile and the struggle for workers' power ★ Phil Marshall: Bookwatch: Islamic activism in the Middle East ★

International Socialism 2:59 Summer 1993
Ann Rogers: Back to the workhouse ★ Kevin Corr and Andy Brown: The labour aristocracy and the roots of reformism ★ Brian Manning: God, Hill and Marx ★ Henry Maitles: Cutting the wire: a criticial appraisal of Primo Levi ★ Hazel Croft: Bookwatch: women and work ★

International Socialism 2:58 Spring 1993
Chris Harman: Where is capitalism going? (part one) ★ Ruth Brown and Peter Morgan: Politics and the class struggle today: a roundtable discussion ★ Richard Greeman: The return of Comrade Tulayev: Victor Serge and the tragic vision of Stalinism ★ Norah Carlin: A new English revolution ★ John Charlton: Building a new world ★ Colin Barker: A reply to Dave McNally ★

International Socialism 2:57 Winter 1992
Lindsey German: Can there be a revolution in Britain? ★ Mike Haynes: Columbus, the Americas and the rise of capitalism ★ Mike Gonzalez: The myths of Columbus: a history ★ Paul Foot: Poetry and revolution ★ Alex Callinicos: Rhetoric which cannot conceal a bankrupt theory: a reply to Ernest Mandel ★ Charlie Kimber: Capitalism, cruelty and conquest ★ David McNulty: Comments on Colin Barker's review of Thompson's *Customs in Common* ★

International Socialism 2:56 Autumn 1992
Chris Harman: The Return of the National Question ★ Dave Treece: Why the Earth Summit failed ★ Mike Gonzalez: Can Castro survive? ★ Lee Humber and John Rees: The good old cause—an interview with Christopher Hill ★ Ernest Mandel: The Impasse of Schematic Dogmatism ★

International Socialism 2:55 Summer 1992
Alex Callinicos: Race and class ★ Lee Sustar: Racism and class struggle in the American Civil War era ★ Lindsey German and Peter Morgan: Prospects for socialists—an interview with Tony Cliff ★ Robert Service: Did Lenin lead to Stalin? ★ Samuel Farber: In defence of democratic revolutionary socialism ★ David Finkel: Defending 'October' or sectarian dogmatism? ★ Robin Blackburn: Reply to John Rees ★ John Rees: Dedicated followers of fashion ★ Colin Barker: In praise of custom ★ Sheila McGregor: Revolutionary witness ★

International Socialism 2:54 Spring 1992
Sharon Smith: Twilight of the American dream ★ Mike Haynes: Class and crisis—the transition in eastern Europe ★ Costas Kossis: A miracle without end? Japanese capitalism and the world economy ★ Alex Callinicos: Capitalism and the state system: A reply to Nigel Harris ★ Steven Rose: Do animals have rights? ★ John Charlton: Crime and class in the 18th century ★ John Rees: Revolution, reform and working class culture ★ Chris Harman: Blood simple ★

International Socialism 2:52 Autumn 1991
John Rees: In defence of October ★ Ian Taylor and Julie Waterson: The political crisis in Greece—an interview with Maria Styllou and Panos Garganas ★ Paul McGarr: Mozart, overture to revolution ★ Lee Humber: Class, class consciousness and the English Revolution ★ Derek Howl: The legacy of Hal Draper ★

International Socialism 2:51 Summer 1991
Chris Harman: The state and capitalism today ★ Alex Callinicos: The end of nationalism? ★ Sharon Smith: Feminists for a strong state? ★ Colin Sparks and Sue Cockerill: Goodbye to the Swedish miracle ★ Simon Phillips: The South African Communist Party and the South African working class ★ John Brown: Class conflict and the crisis of feudalism ★

International Socialism 2:49 Winter 1990
Chris Bambery: The decline of the Western Communist Parties ★ Ernest Mandel: A theory which has not withstood the test of time ★ Chris Harman: Criticism which does not withstand the test of logic ★ Derek Howl: The law of value In the USSR ★ Terry Eagleton: Shakespeare and the class struggle ★ Lionel Sims: Rape and pre-state societies ★ Sheila McGregor: A reply to Lionel Sims ★

International Socialism 2:48 Autumn 1990
Lindsey German: The last days of Thatcher ★ John Rees: The new imperialism ★ Neil Davidson and Donny Gluckstein: Nationalism and the class struggle in Scotland ★ Paul McGarr: Order out of chaos ★

International Socialism 2:46 Winter 1989
Chris Harman: The storm breaks ★ Alex Callinicos: Can South Africa be reformed? ★ John Saville: Britain, the Marshall Plan and the Cold War ★ Sue Clegg: Against the stream ★ John Rees: The rising bourgeoisie ★

International Socialism 2:45 Autumn 1989
Sheila McGregor: Rape, pornography and capitalism ★ Boris Kagarlitsky: The market instead of democracy? ★ Chris Harman: From feudalism to capitalism ★ plus Mike Gonzalez and Sabby Sagall discuss Central America ★

International Socialism 2:44 Autumn 1989
Charlie Hore: China: Tiananmen Square and after ★ Sue Clegg: Thatcher and the welfare state ★ John Molyneux: *Animal Farm* revisited ★ David Finkel: After Arias, is the revolution over? ★ John Rose: Jews in Poland ★

International Socialism 2:43 Summer 1989 (Reprint—special price £4.50)
Marxism and the Great French Revolution by Paul McGarr and Alex Callinicos

International Socialism 2:42 Spring 1989
Chris Harman: The myth of market socialism ★ Norah Carlin: Roots of gay oppression ★ Duncan Blackie: Revolution in science ★ International Socialism Index ★

International Socialism 2:41 Winter 1988
Polish socialists speak out: Solidarity at the Crossroads ★ Mike Haynes: Nightmares of the market ★ Jack Robertson: Socialists and the unions ★ Andy Strouthous: Are the unions in decline? ★ Richard Bradbury: What is Post-Structuralism? ★ Colin Sparks: George Bernard Shaw ★

International Socialism 2:39 Summer 1988
Chris Harman and Andy Zebrowski: Glasnost, before the storm ★ Chanie Rosenberg: Labour and the fight against fascism ★ Mike Gonzalez: Central America after the Peace Plan ★ Ian Birchall: Raymond Williams ★ Alex Callinicos: Reply to John Rees ★

International Socialism 2:35 Summer 1987
Pete Green: Capitalism and the Thatcher years ★ Alex Callinicos: Imperialism, capitalism and the state today ★ Ian Birchall: Five years of *New Socialist* ★ Callinicos and Wood debate 'Looking for alternatives to reformism' ★ David Widgery replies on 'Beating Time' ★

International Socialism 2:31 Winter 1985
Alex Callinicos: Marxism and revolution In South Africa ★ Tony Cliff: The tragedy of A J Cook ★ Nigel Harris: What to do with London? The strategies of the GLC ★

International Socialism 2:30 Autumn 1985
Gareth Jenkins: Where is the Labour Party heading? ★ David McNally: Debt, inflation and the rate of profit ★ Ian Birchall: The terminal crisis in the British Communist Party ★ replies on Women's oppression and *Marxism Today* ★

International Socialism 2:29 Summer 1985
Special issue on the class struggle and the left in the aftermath of the miners' defeat ★ Tony Cliff: Patterns of mass strike ★ Chris Harman: 1984 and the shape of things to come ★ Alex Callinicos: The politics of *Marxism Today* ★

International Socialism 2:26 Spring 1985
Pete Green: Contradictions of the American boom ★ Colin Sparks: Labour and imperialism ★ Chris Bambery: Marx and Engels and the unions ★ Sue Cockerill: The municipal road to socialism ★ Norah Carlin: Is the family part of the superstructure? ★ Kieran Allen: James Connolly and the 1916 rebellion ★

International Socialism 2:25 Autumn 1984
John Newsinger: Jim Larkin, Syndicalism and the 1913 Dublin Lockout ★ Pete Binns: Revolution and state capitalism in the Third World ★ Colin Sparks: Towards a police state? ★ Dave Lyddon: Demystifying the downturn ★ John Molyneux: Do working class men benefit from women's oppression? ★

International Socialism 2:18 Winter 1983
Donny Gluckstein: Workers' councils in Western Europe ★ Jane Ure Smith: The early Communist press in Britain ★ John Newsinger: The Bolivian Revolution ★ Andy Durgan: Largo Caballero and Spanish socialism ★ M Barker and A Beezer: Scarman and the language of racism ★

International Socialism 2:14 Winter 1981
Chris Harman: The riots of 1981 ★ Dave Beecham: Class struggle under the Tories ★ Tony Cliff: Alexandra Kollontai ★ L James and A Paczuska: Socialism needs feminism ★ reply to Cliff on Zetkin ★ Feminists In the labour movement ★

International Socialism 2:13 Summer 1981
Chris Harman: The crisis last time ★ Tony Cliff: Clara Zetkin ★ Ian Birchall: Left Social Democracy In the French Popular Front ★ Pete Green: Alternative Economic Strategy ★ Tim Potter: The death of Eurocommunism ★

International Socialism 2:12 Spring 1981
Jonathan Neale: The Afghan tragedy ★ Lindsey German: Theories of patriarchy ★ Ray Challinor: McDouall and Physical Force Chartism ★ S Freeman & B Vandesteeg: Unproductive labour ★ Alex Callinicos: Wage labour and capitalism ★ Italian fascism ★ Marx's theory of history ★ Cabral ★

International Socialism 2:11 Winter 1980
Rip Bulkeley et al: CND In the 50s ★ Marx's theory of crisis and its critics ★ Andy Durgan: Revolutionary anarchism in Spain ★ Alex Callinicos: Politics or abstract thought ★ Fascism in Europe ★ Marilyn Monroe ★